CREATIVE WRITING

Dianne Doubtfire

Hodder & Stoughton

A MEMBER OF THE HODDER HEADLINE GROUP

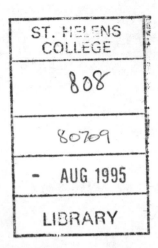

British Library Cataloguing in Publication Data
A Catalogue for this title is available from the British Library

ISBN 0 340 28765 9

First published 1992

Impression number 23 22 21 20 19 18 17 16 15 14
Year   1999 1998 1997 1996 1995

Printed in Great Britain for Hodder & Stoughton Educational, a division of Hodder
Headline Plc, 338 Euston Road, London NW1 3BH by Cox & Wyman Ltd, Reading,
Berkshire.

To my husband Stanley
with all my love

Contents

Foreword   x

Acknowledgments   xii

Introduction   1

1 Developing your Talent   3
Writing for love – and money. What are your
chances? The three stages.

2 How to Write an Article   8
What *is* an article? Choosing a subject.
Market study. A step-by-step guide.
Payment. Illustrations. Some don'ts.

3 The Radio Talk   15

4 Working Arrangements   18
A place to write. Finding the time. Tools of
the trade. Reference books.

5 Presentation of Manuscripts   23
General advice. Articles and short stories.

6 The Short Story   30
Nothing is wasted. The ingredients. Twenty
common faults. Some classic openings.

7 The Radio Story   39

 8 **The Practical Approach**   42
Getting started. Revision.

 9 **Characterisation**   47
Creating believable characters. Choosing
names. How much description?

10 **Dialogue**   52

11 **Setting**   57

12 **Style**   62
Your style is you. The enemies of good style.
Be wary of adjectives.

13 **Poetry**   69
Construction. The Haiku. Presentation of
poetry.

14 **The Non-Fiction Book**   76
Know your subject. Textbooks. Travel books.
Biography. Autobiography. Collaboration.
Presentation of manuscripts.

15 **How to Conduct an Interview**   84

16 **The Novel**   87
The challenge. The theme. The central
character. Setting. Construction. Dramatising
a situation. Presentation of manuscripts.

17 **Writing for Children**   95
The readership. Fiction. Non-fiction. The
under-sevens. Young adults.

18 **Plays**   103
The stage play. The radio play. Television
drama. Presentation of manuscripts.

19 **Finding Titles**   117

20 **Editors, Publishers and Literary Agents**   120

21 Writers' Circles   127

22 The Professional Approach   131
   Twelve points for new writers. Libel. Income
   tax. Copyright. Quotations. Complimentary
   copies. The need for perseverance.

Bibliography   137

Index of Authors Quoted   141

Foreword

The life of the professional writer is an enviable one to many people. To some it even possesses an aura of glamour. Seeing one's work in print or on the television screen; mixing with well-known actors and actresses, mingling with admiring readers at lectures and literary luncheons; being – if one is exceptionally fortunate – handsomely rewarded financially as well. But such moments are bought and paid for by the unremitting labour – year in, year out – of getting words on to paper.

The writer spends most of his working life alone. Not for him the thrill of scoring the winning goal before forty thousand fans, nor the excitement of urging chorus and orchestra through the last movement of Beethoven's Ninth. When the laughter and applause break out in the theatre – or the tears are shed – it's the actors and actresses who are up there onstage. The writer is probably elsewhere, probably already sweating over his next work, while consoling himself – if that is his way – with the knowledge that without him none of it would have happened.

Consoling oneself is the part-time occupation of most writers. Consoling oneself that the book wasn't half-bad after all; that there were *some* good reviews; that there's always a next time. Consoling oneself, more than anything, with the knowledge that there is no justice in the writing world: that some lousy writers make fortunes, while many very good ones earn incomes that make the dole look lavish.

Dianne Doubtfire knows all this: it permeates all the

sound, practical advice she offers in her stimulating book. What she *doesn't* offer is a magic formula, a golden short cut to the glittering prizes. There is none. But any beginner who reads and digests what Mrs Doubtfire has to say will acquire a firm foundation on which to build, and save him or herself a lot of needless disappointment and heartache.

In talking to hundreds of aspirants over the years, I have been struck by how many of them were searching for the basic knowledge needed for getting started along the right road to the writing of good work that someone might be interested enough to buy. And I have wondered why no one wrote an up-to-date book in which all that information was presented for easy assimilation.

Here it is now. It is my pleasure to commend it.

Stan Barstow

Acknowledgments

The author and publishers are grateful to the following authors, publishers, agents and literary executors for permission to include copyright material:

Richard Adams, *Watership Down*: Richard Adams, Rex Collings and David Higham Associates Ltd; H. E. Bates, 'Mr Penfold' from *Thirty-one Selected Tales*: The Estate of the late H. E. Bates, Jonathan Cape Ltd and Laurence Pollinger Ltd; *The Jacaranda Tree* and Preface to *The Modern Short Story*: The Estate of the late H. E. Bates, Michael Joseph Ltd and Laurence Pollinger Ltd; Ian J. Burton, two *haiku*; Sam Butterfield, *Fly Kite*: Roy Butterfield and *The Guardian*; Roald Dahl, 'Beware of the Dog' from *Over To You*: Penguin Books Ltd and Murray Pollinger; Dianne Doubtfire, *The Craft of Novel-Writing*: Allison and Busby Ltd; Margaret Drabble, *The Needle's Eye*: Margaret Drabble and Weidenfeld & Nicolson; T. S. Eliot, 'Tradition and the Individual Talent' from *Selected Essays*: Faber & Faber Ltd and Harcourt Brace Jovanovich Inc; John Fowles, *The French Lieutenant's Woman*: Copyright © John Fowles 1969, reprinted by permission of Jonathan Cape Ltd and Anthony Sheil Associates Ltd; Nadine Gordimer, Introduction to *Selected Stories*: Copyright © 1975 by Nadine Gordimer, reprinted by permission of Viking Penguin Inc and Jonathan Cape Ltd; 'A Mad One' from *A Soldier's Embrace*: Copyright © 1980 by Nadine Gordimer, reprinted by permission of Viking Penguin Inc and Jonathan Cape Ltd; John Hersey, *The War Lover*: Copyright © by John Hersey, reprinted by permission of Hamish Hamilton Ltd and Alfred Knopf Inc; Gerard Manley Hopkins, 'Pied Beauty' from *The Poems of Gerard Manley Hopkins*: fourth edition edited by W. H. Gardner and N. H. MacKenzie, published by Oxford University

Press for the Society of Jesus; P. D. James, *An Unsuitable Job for a Woman*: Copyright © 1972 P. D. James, reprinted with the permission of Charles Scribner's Sons and Faber and Faber Publishers; Tessa Krailing, *A Dinosaur Called Minerva*: Hippo Books (Scholastic) 1980; Laurie Lee, 'Juniper' in *The Sun My Monument*: Laurie Lee and Chatto and Windus Ltd; C. Day Lewis, 'A Happy View' from *Collected Poems 1954*: The Executors of the Estate of C. Day Lewis, Jonathan Cape Ltd and the Hogarth Press; Ian McEwan, *The Cement Garden*: Ian McEwan, Jonathan Cape Ltd and Simon & Schuster Inc; Iris Murdoch, *Nuns and Soldiers*: Copyright © 1980 by Iris Murdoch, reprinted by permission of Viking Penguin Inc and Chatto and Windus Ltd; Edna O'Brien, 'The Love Object' from *The Love Object*: Edna O'Brien, Jonathan Cape Ltd, Alfred Knopf Inc and Robert Lescher; Colin Oliver, *haiku*: Shollond Publications; Jill Paton Walsh, a statement made to the author; Sylvia Plath, 'Insomniac' from *Crossing the Water*: Copyright © Ted Hughes 1971, reprinted by permission of Faber & Faber Ltd and Olwyn Hughes; Roy Russell, part of a letter to the author; Vernon Scannell, 'Cold Spell' from *The Winter Man*: Allison & Busby Ltd; Dylan Thomas, 'The force that through the green fuse drives the flower' from *Collected Poems*: Executors of the Estate of Dylan Thomas, J. M. Dent and David Higham Associates Ltd; Alan W. Watts, *The Way of Zen*: Thames & Hudson Ltd and Pantheon Books, a division of Random House Inc; Dorothy Wright, *The Homecoming*; Interview with Anne Sexton from *Writers at Work: The Paris Review Interviews* (Fourth Series), edited by George Plimpton: Copyright © 1974, 1976 by The Paris Review, Inc, reprinted by permission of Viking Penguin Inc and Martin Secker & Warburg Ltd.

The author and publishers also acknowledge the use of quotations from BBC Publications; Lewis Carroll; G. K. Chesterton; Joseph Conrad; *Fowler's Modern English Usage*; Christopher Fry; Robert Graves; Aldous Huxley; Samuel Johnson; Nicholas Monsarrat; Pirandello; William Shakespeare; Robert Louis Stevenson; Anton Tchekov; Evelyn Waugh; Thornton Wilder.

The author would also like to extend warm personal thanks to the following, who suggested improvements: Stan Barstow; Dorothy Branco; Ian J. Burton; Ashley Doubtfire; Stanley Doubtfire; Ann Hoffmann; Susan Newell; Roy Russell; Elizabeth Stevens; Marjorie Tepper; Constance White; the members of the Isle of Wight New Writers' Group. Also to Ruth Kimber, former Editor of Teach Yourself Books, who invited her to write this book in the first place, and to Joan Maynard who typed the final manuscript with such speed and efficiency.

Introduction

Creative writing must surely be one of the most satisfying occupations in the world, and as with everything else, the greater your skill the more enjoyable your work becomes. When studied seriously, as it deserves to be, it is extremely demanding, but the rewards – in pleasure and often in money – are well worth the effort.

You will have your own special reasons for picking up this book. Perhaps you have no wish to see your work in print but only want to write for your own private enjoyment, setting down your thoughts and experiences, revelling in the beauty of words. Whatever your goal may be – fame, money, therapy or the need to express and communicate ideas – it is vital for you to study your craft if you are to make the best use of your time. You will write in your own individual way, developing your own style, but every piece of writing, whether it is a poem, a letter to the local paper or a novel of a hundred thousand words, must have a *shape*. To master the art of construction requires dedication and sustained effort. '*Success*', wrote Evelyn Waugh, '*depends on natural talent developed by hard work.*'

I have been writing professionally for nearly thirty years but I still revise a great deal. This page you are reading was rewritten and retyped eight times before I was satisfied that I had expressed myself clearly, saying what I wished to say, no more, no less. An introduction must contain enough to persuade the reader to continue, but not so much that he or she becomes discouraged.

I hope you won't be discouraged. There is endless satisfaction to be gained from putting your ideas on paper as best you can and going on from there to improve what you have written. We may come very close to perfection, sometimes in a flash of inspiration but usually after a lot of hard work; those are the occasions that delight and renew us, enabling us to face the days of trial and error which are also a part of the task.

Even if you are a complete beginner, an idea you jot down today on the back of an old envelope could be the basis for an influential article or even a best-selling novel, but you will need to learn the techniques in order to develop your idea to the best advantage. It is rare for anyone to succeed as a writer without a considerable amount of experience. There can be no set rules, only guidelines, but the novice would do well to follow them until he can break them with wisdom and panache, possibly producing a masterpiece. Whenever I say 'he' I mean, of course, 'he or she'; what a pity it is that the English language, with all its depth and subtlety, has left us without a personal pronoun which includes both sexes!

It is advisable to study this book as a whole. It would have been impossible for me to arrange all the information in watertight compartments even if I had wished to do so; Creative Writing has so many varied aspects, mingled and inter-related. Characterisation, for instance, is as vital to the short story and the play as it is to the novel; planning, construction and good style are always necessary; so is revision.

Whatever your goal, I hope this book will help you to reach it with maximum speed and enormous enjoyment.

Dianne Doubtfire

1

Developing your Talent

Writing for love – and money

This book is designed primarily for the new writer who
wishes to see his or her work in print; most beginners feel the
need to communicate their ideas and to receive the proper
rewards. Those who have no such ambitions, however, will
learn to improve their writing and thereby take more pride
and pleasure in it.

People sometimes think that there are two kinds of
writers, clearly defined and poles apart: those who write for
love and those who write for money. There are the sensitive,
artistic writers on the one hand, they say, men and women of
integrity who would rather die than 'prostitute their art', and
on the other hand there are the hard-headed commercial
hacks who write for money and money only, and will
produce any kind of trash provided there is a big cheque at
the end of it. This, of course, is nonsense. It is not only
possible but desirable to write for love and money at the
same time; the two aims can complement one another.

The secret of success is twofold: firstly to discover, by trial
and error, the branch of writing which is right for you, and
secondly to master your craft so that you can produce the
best you are capable of in your chosen field. To write for lov̸
as well as money you must reach a high standard *for ̸*
own satisfaction and not just in order to sell you̸
remember the late and lovable L. A. G. Stron̸
great vehemence at a writers' conference in ̸
grave mistake, even from a financial point of ̸

with only money as your goal. Those who write from the heart with dedication and sincerity, he said, are far more likely to win fame and fortune. Their writings will endure because the perceptive reader recognises sincerity and warms to it, remembering the author's name and seeking out his work. No one can deny, of course, that there is big money to be made from novels which exploit the undoubted appeal of sex and violence, but firstly, whatever kind of book you want to write, get down to work and learn your trade. A gifted and experienced writer can handle any theme and stamp it with lasting literary quality.

Needless to say, I profoundly disagree with Samuel Johnson when he pronounces that '*No man but a blockhead ever wrote, except for money*'. To prove the fallacy of this – if proof were needed – we have only to think of the millions of children, all over the world, who produce their poems and stories with no thought of payment. Are we to believe that in adult life they suddenly turn into blockheads if they continue to write on impulse for no other reason than their own delight?

What are your chances?

This book can only present my personal views, wide open, of course, for discussion and possible disagreement, but the following qualities seem to embrace the essentials for success: Talent – Sincerity – Technique – Perseverence. 'But how about luck?' you may ask. 'Isn't it *who* you know that really counts? Or whether you happen to get your book to a publisher ahead of someone else with a similar idea?' It's certainly true that timing, choice of subject, and the personal preferences of people at the top can be propitious or otherwise. You may happen to meet an editor at a party, get talking over a drink, tell him about your ambitions and hear him say: 'It sounds as if you might be able to fill a slot for us – how about lunch next week to discuss it?' It *does* happen, but very seldom. And where would you be if your work wasn't up to standard? I think you should forget about ιck, both good and bad, and simply get on with the all-sorbing task of teaching yourself to write.

How can you tell if you possess the necessary talent? Most potential writers have an instinctive love of words and a gift for stringing them together. They earned high marks at school for English and probably kept a diary or wrote poetry in their childhood. (Incidentally, they often have trouble with figures; I once got two marks out of a hundred for arithmetic!) Potential fiction-writers usually write long chatty letters to their friends, have a tendency to exaggerate, and talk to themselves a good deal. They often have a talent for pictorial art. It is also likely that they suffered in their youth at the hands of parents or teachers who couldn't understand the dream-world of the imagination which beguiled them away from more mundane activities. Can I hear you saying, 'Yes, that's *me*!'? Then what are you waiting for? People will always delight in a good story, and a regular influx of new writers is constantly in demand, whatever the economic climate.

Even so, there is far less fiction published than non-fiction – five or six times less – so if you are a factual person you have particularly favourable prospects. Nature books, travelogues, biographies and how-to-do-it books are ever popular; it's just a matter of using your knowledge and experience to the best advantage. Non-fiction writers have a practical turn of mind. They enjoy research and take pleasure in the orderly assembly of facts. They often find it difficult to create characters and invent situations, preferring to keep their feet firmly on the ground. Imaginative writers may write excellent non-fiction, but unfortunately the reverse is seldom true. Factual people sometimes have the false idea that it is more prestigious to write novels, and insist on trying fiction even though they are continually drawn towards real-life situations rather than imaginary ones. Fiction and non-fiction are of equal importance; it's the quality that counts. So follow your natural bent and don't be tempted to go against the grain.

The three stages

There are three stages in every writer's life. The first is one of blissful ignorance. You write for pleasure, freely expressing yourself, quite satisfied – even delighted – with what you are doing, although it may be shapeless, wordy and full of irrelevancies. Some people, writing alone without guidance, never advance beyond this stage.

The second stage arrives when you join a Writer's Circle, attend a course on Creative Writing, or read a book like this. You discover with a pang of dismay that there is a great deal more to this writing game than you ever dreamed of, and that although your work may be 'promising' you have a lot to learn and it won't be easy. You see your mistakes as if they had suddenly appeared in block capitals, but you have no idea – or very little – how to put them right. That beautifully sensitive and atmospheric short story you wrote last month isn't a short story at all, you discover; it's a sort of hybrid sketch-cum-anecdote with no beginning, middle and end – at least, not in that order!

At this stage the novice, torn between the longing to express himself spontaneously and the need to be published, is inclined to fight shy of the whole project. This is quite understandable. He is deeply disappointed to learn that his work is full of faults when he had thought it reasonably accomplished. He feels inadequate, and the fear of failure is hard to dispel. If you are faced with this dilemma, take heart from the certainty that most professional writers have felt exactly the same. I know I did. This is the stage which will determine your future as a writer, so don't give up. I wrote fifty-seven short stories before I had one accepted, and later went on to publish twelve novels and four non-fiction books. If you plan your campaign with confidence and optimism you have every chance of success. I've had students who made such progress that they received cheques for articles and short stories while they were still attending my classes. Of course it's exceptional to sell your work so soon, but a talented person who is eager to learn, ruthlessly self-critical and prepared for sustained effort can achieve success remarkably quickly. Stage two can last for months or for years, depending on your determination.

Stage three brings true satisfaction. Now you can see your faults and you know how to correct them. You understand exactly how to revise your work – pruning, rearranging, discarding, polishing – until you have produced a piece of writing, be it long or short, fiction or non-fiction, which satisfies your newly-acquired high standards and will be likely to please an editor. There will always be a gap between the dream you cherish and the best you are capable of, but this is surely a part of the joy – the striving for an elusive perfection, the gradual improvement and the ever-growing sense of power over words. 'They're all there in the dictionary,' someone quipped at me when I was an unsuccessful beginner, 'all you've got to do is sort 'em out.' That was the day I might have given up, but we all have to contend with the pessimists who will try to warn us off or ridicule our enthusiasm. You must disregard them and work with care and confidence towards your goal.

Exercise 1

Write a short anecdote (300–500 words) with the title 'Seen Through a Window', describing what is seen and the feelings of the person looking. This person may be you or someone imaginary. Similarly, whatever is seen may be real or fictitious. This is a valuable exercise as it gives the student experience in writing about emotions as well as the outside world. The window frame provides a boundary and the writer who keeps within that boundary will learn the vital discipline of restraint. The reader's attention will be concentrated in such a way that he will be looking through that window himself and sharing the feelings of the viewpoint character.

Here are a few examples: a tramp looking into a luxurious drawing room; a child looking into a doll's house; a fireman on his ladder looking into a burning room; a bed-ridden woman looking out of the window at the garden she used to tend; a man looking in a shop window at something he longs to buy but cannot afford.

My students have always enjoyed this exercise and of course there is no end to the number of times it may be attempted. On many occasions the resulting piece has formed the basis for a short story and has even sparked off a successful novel.

2

How to Write an Article

What *is* an article?

An article is not fiction, although it might contain semi-fictitious anecdotes or imaginary dialogue to illustrate certain points. It is a factual piece, sometimes described as a feature, and usually conveys information (Take your Caravan to Spain; How to Make a Deck-chair; Better Health through Autosuggestion; Choosing Music for an Amateur Film). If you want to be published you must avoid the essay-type article which is reminiscent of a school composition, describing a personal experience or a private opinion. If the situation is really outstanding it could be a winner, but it is a sad fact that the general reader has little interest in our ordinary activities, however well we describe them. Moving house, holidays that went wrong, opinions on the social ills of the day, etc., are usually non-starters. If you are a well-known personality, of course, all that is changed: a popular disc-jockey could write about what he had for breakfast last Tuesday and get away with it! Letters to newspapers and magazines are an exception; here the new writer stands a good chance of getting his personal views into print if he can express himself in a lively way, with every superfluous word cut out and no deviation from the main point. Excellent practice, in fact, for the potential article-writer. Letters are paid for only when the periodical says so on the 'Letters' page.

Journalism cannot be included in a book on Creative Writing as it consists chiefly of factual reporting, but there are several books available on the subject (see Bibliography).

The best way to learn how to write is to *write*, so why not begin an article at once? You have only to look at the variety of magazines on display at a station bookstall to realise that there is a constant demand for new material. Most journals buy work from freelances although regular features are done by staff writers. Study the list of newspapers and magazines in the current *Writers' and Artists' Yearbook* (published annually by A. & C. Black) to find their requirements. You will be encouraged to discover that there are about seven hundred of them!

Choosing a subject

Successful articles usually fall under one of three headings:

1   A subject about which the writer has specialised knowledge (Beekeeping; Zambia; Teaching Deaf Children; Roman Britain; Water-colour Painting; Vegan Cookery).
2   An unusual slant on an ordinary subject. (A holiday in Paris is obviously too commonplace, but if you wrote a piece comparing the Paris Metro with the London Underground you might be successful.)
3   Humour. If you can write a really funny – and I mean hilarious – article, almost *any* subject is suitable (Don't let your wife teach you to drive; The first time I baby-sat; How to gain weight without even trying).

If you are short of ideas at this stage, try a topical theme. This will entail research if you are not already an expert on your chosen subject. You could interview a well-known writer for the publication day of his latest book (see Chapter 15), write something for the centenary of the death of some famous personage, perhaps with local connections, or work out a humorous piece for Hallowe'en. You will find that the more articles you write, the more readily ideas will come to you. When you read a magazine you will say to yourself 'Why didn't *I* think of that?', and never a day will pass without some intriguing new subject presenting itself. Jot your ideas down quickly (they can soon be lost if you don't) and once you have learnt the technique of constructing a well-written, entertaining article you may find that you can sell your work quite easily.

Market study

It is essential to study the journals you wish to write for. This should be self-evident but it is remarkable how often it is overlooked. I know a man who sent an article on Karate to a genteel magazine for ladies. 'They should all learn how to defend themselves,' he said. The magazines you choose for market study will usually be the ones you enjoy reading, the ones which specialise in your particular interests. Study the length, style and content of every article in several *recent* issues (editors and policies are frequently changing) and make a note of your findings. You will discover that the length of an article can be anything from 300 to 3000 words or more. A good average is 1500. Articles of less than 500 words are usually classed as 'fillers' and are used to occupy odd spaces at the bottom of the page. The *Writers' and Artists' Yearbook* gives a list of magazines which accept filler paragraphs.

A step-by-step guide

1   Choose your subject, making sure that it falls under one of the three headings listed previously. It must be a theme that really interests you, otherwise you cannot hope to engage your reader.

2   Select a possible market, even though you are as yet unpractised; a definite goal will give you an incentive to make a determined effort, and – who knows? – you might be successful with your first attempt. Professional writers nearly always decide on a market for their articles and short stories before they begin to plan them.

3   Think out all the possible angles on your subject and make a rough list, in any order.

4   Sort out the best, discarding any points which are repetitive or not strictly related to the subject.

5   Decide whether you need more information and, if you do, take a notebook to your reference library.

6   Plan what order your points should take, bearing in mind that the opening must have real impact. It is sometimes a good idea to begin with a question which involves the reader at the outset. The various points you have jotted down must now be arranged in a logical sequence so that the paragraphs flow smoothly towards a strong ending; this means you should save your most vital point till last. Finally you can sum up, *very briefly*, what the piece is about.

7   Write the first draft, improving on your original plan where necessary. When you have written the whole article you will see more clearly how to prune it and rearrange it. Be sure to cut out everything that might be described as 'waffle'. This is the way to streamline your prose and keep the reader's interest.

8   Choose a short, snappy title (see Chapter 19).

9   Verify all your facts, making sure they are up to date. Editors trust their contributors to maintain a high standard of accuracy and you must always be reliable in every way if you want to go on selling your work.

10   Keep on rewriting until you are satisfied that you have done all you can to improve it. Never say, 'Oh, I can't do it *again*!' Revision is essential, however tedious. It is always difficult to retain the original spontaneity while slaving to polish your work, but experience will gradually teach you how to do it. This is one of the greatest problems any writer has to face.

If you belong to a Writers' Circle (and I strongly recommend it) now is the time to take your article along for criticism. You won't agree with every verdict, but you will certainly receive some helpful advice. We all get so close to our work that we need a fresh opinion, especially after many hours of revision.

11   When you feel that your article is ready for submission, type it – or have it typed – in double spacing on A4 paper, following the advice laid down in Chapter 5. Pay great attention to detail; editors are highly professional people and they like their contributors to have an equally professional approach.

12   Be sure to submit a topical article in good time: a week ahead for dailies; two to three months for a weekly; four to seven months for a monthly. I was surprised to learn, when I was a beginner, that some editors buy their Christmas articles in June.

Payment

Fees vary a great deal, depending largely on the circulation of the journal. Naturally, a well-known writer can claim a higher fee than a beginner, but otherwise payment is much the same for everyone, increasing if you become a regular contributor. Cheques are usually sent out after publication but some journals pay on acceptance.

If your work is worthy of publication it is worthy of payment, and let no one persuade you otherwise. In fairness to other writers you should demand a proper fee, no matter how strongly you might feel that you would gladly let them have it for nothing just to see it in print. Be courteous but firm in all your dealings with editors. Don't allow fear of rejection to coerce you into accepting shoddy treatment. Most editors are fair and reasonable but some will take advantage of an inexperienced writer. It happened to me.

I had sold five articles to a glossy magazine (now defunct). Not long after the fifth one appeared in print I met a professional writer who had contributed to the same magazine. She said she had enjoyed my pieces and added, 'By the way, how much are they paying you?' When I told her, she was aghast. It transpired that she received three times that rate from the same magazine. 'Next time, you must ask for more money', she said. I was afraid they might drop me if I did, but she insisted that I must never again accept this meagre sum (which had seemed to me quite princely).

I sent them another article, and when they accepted it, offering the usual payment, I nervously composed a letter saying that I thought a certain sum (three times as much) was 'a more appropriate fee'. I think that letter took me almost as long to write as the original article! I needn't have worried; they agreed like lambs and I continued to sell them my work at the new rate.

Illustrations

Don't attempt to do your own illustrations unless you are an exceptionally talented artist. Even then, you may find that your editor prefers to use his Art Department. Sketches and diagrams, however, could be useful for the guidance of a staff artist.

Good black-and-white photographs might well improve your chances of success. Submit only prints; *never* send negatives. Photos must be glossy with plenty of contrast, and no smaller than half plate (16½ × 12 cm, or 6½″ × 4¾″). Label them on the back with gummed paper; don't write on the print itself. Pack carefully with stiff cardboard.

If you have high-quality colour transparencies on no account send them with the article, but enclose a covering letter giving details, including size: 6 × 6 cm is the most suitable, but 35 mm is sometimes acceptable. If the editor likes your article he will probably ask to see the slides.

It doesn't matter if you have no photographs; editors can obtain suitable pictures from an agency. Incidentally, if your own photographs are used you should receive extra payment.

Some don'ts

Don't state the obvious ('Rain can be a disaster or a blessing'; 'After-dinner speakers are often boring').
Don't combine two or more subjects. This not only wastes material but spoils your article.
Don't preach.
Don't pad. If your article isn't long enough for the market,

write it up for a different magazine or choose a subject with more 'meat' in it.

Don't repeat yourself. The reader will lose interest unless every sentence is new and fresh.

Don't be pessimistic. No one wants to feel dejected at the end of an article, and editors want to sell their magazines. If you are expressing a grievance be sure to present a positive remedy.

Don't 'embroider' your prose for the sake of poetic imagery or to include some anecdote which has special significance for you but might bore the reader. (This advice is often hard to follow; you may need an honest colleague to point out these passages.)

Don't hesitate to rewrite the whole article as many times as necessary.

Don't be discouraged by setbacks. Most writers have collected dozens of rejection slips by the time they reach the professional stage; one of my friends has actually papered the loo with them!

Exercise 2

Write an article of about 1000 words on a subject of your choice, having in mind a suitable market.

3

The Radio Talk

A talk for radio must be specially written for the medium. Although it is like an article in many ways, it must be framed in a lively, conversational style, as if you were chatting to a friend; it's no use sending a rejected magazine article to the BBC in the hope that it 'might do as a talk'. On the other hand, rewritten for broadcasting, it might well be successful.

According to the booklet *Writing for the BBC*, '*scripts should be written for reading aloud and thus have a simple and direct construction without long literary sub-clauses or strings of adjectives . . . The best talks are often those where the writer is burning to communicate some idea or recount some experience.*' It is particularly important to prepare an arresting opening; the listener will soon switch off if he is not immediately attracted by what you have to say and the way you say it. You will need to use fairly short sentences and develop a colloquial turn of phrase, abbreviating 'would not' into 'wouldn't', 'cannot' into 'can't', etc., in order to give your talk the right degree of intimacy. For instance, in an article you may write: 'I was very frightened, so much so that my knees were trembling.' This would sound stilted in a talk. Instead, you could say: 'I can't pretend I wasn't scared – I was shaking like a leaf.' Clichés such as 'shaking like a leaf', which are to be avoided in straight narrative, can be included in a talk because we all use them in everyday speech.

Bear in mind that the listener is unable to glance back over the text as the magazine reader can, and therefore your writing must be very clear and explicit. Don't say: 'Standing by the window, fingering his tie, and looking like a nervous schoolboy, stood my old headmaster.' For radio write it straight: 'My old headmaster stood by the window, fingering his tie and looking like a nervous schoolboy.' It is wise to avoid starting a sentence with the present participle, certainly for radio, and indeed on most occasions.

Woman's Hour (which is by no means restricted to women writers) is always ready to consider work by newcomers. Five minutes is a good length (about 800 words). If you can write in a humorous vein you're half way there, and talks which are helpful to listeners are also in demand (e.g. the overcoming of health or emotional problems). These must be written without a trace of self pity or sentimentality, and this, of course, applies to all good writing.

Talks of ten, fifteen, twenty or even thirty minutes are bought by the BBC from freelance writers, but you should study the *Radio Times* for current requirements. Scripts are needed for the regions, for school broadcasting and for current affairs and religious programmes, but you must be qualified to write them and state the details in a covering letter. (For example, for Schools: 'I enclose a ten-minute talk for twelve-year-olds on "Crocodiles of the Nile". I spent the past two years in Egypt studying this subject'.) Local radio provides excellent openings for the new writer. Tune in as often as you can and analyse the programmes to find out what you might contribute.

If you want to write for radio it is essential to study the market by frequent listening. Pay close attention to the kinds of talks which are being transmitted, the length required and the style in which they are written. Read your work aloud before you type it finally; in this way you will be sure that it is conversational rather than literary and also that the timing is correct. The BBC runs efficiently because everyone is geared to think in seconds rather than minutes. Your scripts *must* be accurately timed; read quite slowly with adequate pauses between sentences. Most people are inclined to hurry. Err on the long side rather than the reverse; almost every piece of writing is improved by cutting, but padding can be disastrous.

A cassette recorder is, of course, immensely useful in

radio writing. Some people find they can speak their talks straight onto tape, transcribing and editing them later. This, they feel, ensures a chatty style. For me it would ensure interminable silence, but we all have our special gifts and weaknesses, and must find our different ways accordingly.

Talks are always read over the air by their authors and you will have to undergo a voice test at the microphone before your manuscript can be finally accepted. This is nothing to worry about and most people pass without difficulty. Very occasionally, however, someone's voice may have a certain quality which makes it unsuitable for radio. I knew a woman with a delightful speaking voice but she had a way of pronouncing the letter 's' which caused a slight hissing sound when transmitted, and her talk could not be accepted. Fortunately she was able to rewrite it as an article and sell it to a magazine.

It's natural to feel a little daunted by the prospect of reading your talk to an audience of millions, but don't let the thought of it deter you from submitting a script. Once you are in the studio your 'butterflies' will vanish and you will be amazed to find the occasion really enjoyable.

Exercise 3

Write a five-minute talk for radio, timing it accurately.

4

Working Arrangements

A place to write

A room of one's own is every writer's dream, but few of us can manage it and we must do the best we can with what is available. For fifteen years I wrote on the kitchen table or in a bedroom. Now I am lucky enough to have a garden chalet and never a day goes by when I don't thank heaven for my good fortune.

There is sometimes a spare room which can be converted into a study, otherwise a bedroom might have to be commandeered for use in the daytime. You will need a table (even a folding card table), a good directional light and some form of heating in the winter. I used a paraffin stove. Luckily a writer can function, if he really has to, with nothing but a notebook and a stub of pencil, but some of us do need peace and quiet. I know a woman with a teenage son who is learning to play the trumpet and she escapes in the car, parks it in a secluded road and sits there peacefully writing her articles, resting a clip-board on the steering wheel. Another friend has a difficult husband who pours scorn on her 'scribbling' and upbraids her for wasting her time whenever she picks up a pencil. She writes in the bus station waiting-room. On the way home she buys something nice for supper and tells him there were terrible queues in the supermarket. Another story concerns a man whose wife and mother-in-law watch television non-stop every evening. This is his only chance to write, and his wife makes trouble if he 'litters the house with his papers and all that mess'. His solution is to put a pile of cushions in the bath. There he sits, in comfort and seclusion, writing his novel.

Even without such personal problems, a place to work can be difficult to arrange, but somehow you will find a way if you are really determined.

Finding the time

'Dividing the day into manageable portions', said Robert Louis Stevenson, *'brings peace of mind and healthful activity of body.'* This is what we must do if we are to succeed in the craft of writing. For anyone with a full-time job – and running a home is one of the most demanding of all – it can never be easy to organise the extra time you need. An hour a day will do to begin with, provided it is *regular*. Later you will almost certainly want to give more time to it and something will have to be curtailed – reading, television, gardening, meeting friends. A serious writer, one who is destined for success, is always prepared to make sacrifices. People have often said to me, 'Oh, I know I could write a book if only I had the time!' I nod and say nothing, knowing that the talented and dedicated writer will *make* the time, no matter what the difficulties. After all, if you work for eight hours at some other job and sleep for eight, you still have another eight to play with. Even if you have demanding hobbies, a demanding family and demanding hangers-on, you can surely manage to steal an hour or two for your writing. When my son was small I got up at 4.30 in the morning because that was the only way to find a couple of hours when the house was quiet and I wasn't too tired to concentrate. I still get up at half past five; for me it's the perfect time to work. If you're a late-night person, maybe you could burn a little midnight oil. And if you have been sleeping for eight hours, why not give yourself a three-week trial of managing on seven. I never thought it would work for me, but now I fare much better that way.

Most writers feel that it is incredibly difficult to start, even with plenty of time at their disposal. I find myself writing letters that could easily wait, reading the paper (which always depresses me anyway), varnishing my nails, sorting out recipes – *anything* but getting started. And yet, once I begin, I can hardly bear to stop.

My solution is to remind myself that these wasted minutes will never be returned to me and that if I get some work behind me I shall be happy. 'You'll be *miserable*', I tell myself, 'if you don't get another chapter finished today.' And that's what does it. I don't want to be miserable – especially as a result of my own laziness – and so I go to my study and begin. I aim to work for six hours every day, but even if I only manage a thousand words in that time (and cross out half of them!) I'm satisfied. I've been working towards the end of the book, and trial and error, as I'm always reminding myself and other people, is part of the task. Make your own deadlines until you have an editor or a publisher to make them for you, and try to practise discipline in fulfilling them. Use the time you have set aside, *even if you appear to have nothing to write* (see Nicholas Monsarrat's advice on page 43). This is the way to learn your craft as speedily as possible.

Tools of the trade

You will, of course, need a typewriter, but you can manage without one for a while, if need be, provided you get your work properly typed for submission. If you are buying a new machine I would suggest that you choose elite type. It is in popular use and because the letters are smaller than pica you will save a lot of paper over the years. Avoid the fancy typeface which imitates longhand; editors hate it.

It is a great advantage to do your own typing. Even though you may always write your first draft in longhand, as I do, it is helpful to 'see it in print' as it were, to get a correct impression of your paragraphing and the general look of the thing. Besides, you will find that you can improve your work as you type it out; that's why many well-known writers who could easily afford a secretary, employ a professional typist only for the final version.

On your desk, if you have one (or in a drawer or a box if you are working on a table which has to be cleared for meals), you will require the following items:

'Ideas' book for noting down a brainwave the moment it arrives.

Notepad (I use A4 lined tear-off blocks).

Pencils, pencil sharpener and rubber.

Ball-point or fountain pen.

Paper clips.

A4 typing paper and copy paper (in America 11″ × 8½″). It is a good idea to use pastel-tinted copy paper so that you can sort out the pages at a glance.

Carbon paper.

Spare typewriter ribbon.

Typewriter cleaning brush.

Correction strips or fluid.

Scrap paper (offcuts are often sold cheaply by local printers).

Envelopes.

Reference books

There are three books every writer should have on his desk: a good dictionary, *Roget's Thesaurus of English Words and Phrases* and the current edition of *The Writers' and Artists' Yearbook* (in America *The Writer's Handbook*, *The Literary Market Place* or *The Writer's Market*). For quick reference *The Oxford Concise Dictionary* or *The Penguin English Dictionary* are ideal, but you should really have a more extensive one. The following are recommended: *The Shorter Oxford English*; *Collins English*; *Chambers Twentieth Century*; *Longman Modern*; *Webster's New Collegiate*; *Webster's Third New International Dictionary of the English Language*.

The following books are also very useful and may be consulted in most public reference libraries: *Fowler's Modern English Usage* (OUP); *Strunk and White's Elements of Style* (Macmillan); *Brewer's Dictionary of Phrase and Fable* (Cassell); *Chambers' Encyclopaedia*, *Encyclopaedia Britannica* or *Everyman's Encyclopaedia*; *Oxford Dictionary of Quotations* (OUP); *Dictionary of People and Places* (Collins); *The Synonym Finder* (Rodale Press); *Skeat's Concise Etymological Dictionary* (OUP).

Exercise 4

Decide on a place and time to do an hour's writing a day and
put your plans into practice within the next two weeks.

5

Presentation of Manuscripts

General advice

It cannot be too strongly emphasised that your typescript must be impeccable. I have seen a short story which was sent to an editor on flimsy little sheets of blue notepaper, hand-written in purple ink and fastened together with a *pin*! Such extremes are rare, thank goodness, but many beginners send out their MSS in an unbelievably shoddy state. You have put a great deal of work into your writing and it would be madness not to take equal care with its presentation. It's easy to get it right when you understand the requirements.

First of all, your work *must* be typed: very few editors, if any, will even look at longhand material. It is certainly preferable to do it yourself, not only for reasons of economy but because you will want to make improvements as you sort out your scribble.

If you have never done any typing I would strongly advise you to learn to touch-type right from the start. I'm still muddling through with two fingers and although I can rattle away quite fast I wish I had trained myself properly when I began. Maybe I've left it too late, but if you're starting from scratch you could go to evening classes or learn from *Teach Yourself Typewriting*. If you have your work typed by a friend, be sure that he or she is fully aware of the correct layout; typist friends are sometimes set in old-fashioned ways.

A manuscript, in official jargon, is the same thing as a typescript, although the word 'manuscript' implies that it is written by hand (MS = manuscript, plural MSS; p. = page, plural pp.). Use good quality A4 typing paper (297 × 210 mm or 11½″ × 8¼″). Foolscap and quarto sizes are now outdated (in America 11″ × 8½″ is usual).

The layout of your work on the page is extremely important. You should allow a good margin on the left-hand side (not less than 40 mm or 1½″) with at least 25 mm or 1″ top and bottom and 13 mm or ½″ on the right. Be sure that your margins are consistent throughout the typescript. Use one side of the paper only and type in double spacing – i.e. a depth of two lines. (It is advisable to use this same double spacing for your own rough draft as well, to simplify revision; it is almost impossible to make amendments and additions if the work is single spaced.) It is neither necessary nor desirable to allow extra spacing between paragraphs. Be sure to number your pages, preferably in the top right-hand corner, and check that they are in the correct order.

Always take a carbon copy of your work before sending it out, and don't forget to bring your copy up to date with the latest corrections. The loss of a manuscript when there is no carbon can be one of the saddest experiences in a writer's life. A friend of mine lost the only typescript of a whole novel in the post. It was registered, but no amount of money could compensate her for the loss of something so precious and irreplaceable. Never part with a one-and-only version of anything you have written.

You must, of course, keep your alterations to a minimum. It is acceptable to make one or two minor amendments, rather than retype the whole page, but do it with a fine biro in lettering which is as close as possible to typescript. Do not alter in block capitals; if you do, how is the printer to know when you *really* want capitals? Italics are indicated by underlining. If the sentence is already in italics and you wish to emphasise a word, you omit the underlining on that word (e.g. <u>What</u> is <u>an article</u>?).

It is usual to indent five spaces for a new paragraph (unlike an official letter) and to allow two spaces after a full stop. Details such as these are by no means vital to your success as a writer, but it's just as easy to be accurate so why not let your typescript proclaim your general efficiency? Do take care when you need to split a word at the end of a line. It may seem obvious that 'disappointed' should be divided into 'dis-appointed' but, believe it or not, I've seen 'disappointed'!

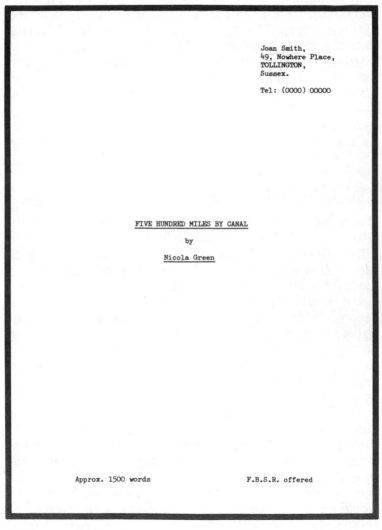

Fig. 5.1 *Specimen layout for the title page of an article or short story*

The title page of every manuscript should bear your name, address and telephone number at the top right-hand side (see Fig. 5.1). About half way down comes the title in capitals and under that the 'by-line'. This is where you give your pseudonym if you want to use one, but I don't advise it unless you have a special reason for not using your real name; it only complicates matters. At the bottom of the page state the approximate number of words. The assessment of wordage is important but there is no need to count every word except for very short pieces. Take an average of six lines, count the number of lines on a page and multiply one by the other. Never state the exact number of words; give it to the nearest hundred for articles and short stories, to the nearest thousand for full-length books. If an editor sees '2832 words' he will know at once that you are a beginner.

Articles and short stories

When you submit stories and articles to periodicals in the UK you should also state at the bottom of your title page: 'First British Serial Rights offered' (or FBSRO). This indicates that you are not prepared to sell the copyright but only the right to publish the piece once only, for the first time in Great Britain. After a few years you might be able to sell the Second British Serial Rights, but when offering second rights always state when and where the material was first published. An article already published in a magazine can sometimes be rewritten as a radio talk from a different angle. 'FBSRO' doesn't apply here because the BBC has its own terms of contract.

The copyright of all your work belongs to you, as the author, unless you agree to sell it (see page 134). This you should seldom do, except perhaps in the case of poetry. Your short story, for instance, may be spotted in a magazine by a film or television company (unlikely but possible) and if you had sold the copyright, the magazine which bought it would get all the money and you might never even know about it. If you are sent a letter or a cheque which implies the purchase of 'the copyright' or 'all rights' simply cross it out and substitute 'FBSR'. You are unlikely to meet with any trouble; it's just one of the things that some editors try to get away with!

So much for the title page. The first page of the actual manuscript (see Fig. 5.2) must bear again, top right, your

---

Joan Smith,
49, Nowhere Place,
TOLLINGTON,
Sussex.

FIVE HUNDRED MILES BY CANAL

by

Nicola Green

'Fancy going in winter!' they said. But that was the way we wanted it. In a tiny cabin cruiser last year, my husband and I covered five hundred miles of the canals of England - from London to Manchester and back - and we found a new country.

We wanted to discover the 'Cut' alone, without the transistors and orange peel of the holiday season. Frosts and snows whitened the roof of our little craft as we nosed our way slowly from lock to lock, from town to town, sometimes hacking a channel through stretches of ice.

We shared those lonely reaches with only the narrow-boats, still chugging along with their various cargoes, and the calm, unhurried scene might have belonged to the 19th century. Between the towns, the canal passed through forests and fields, over tall aqueducts, through dark, dripping tunnels, and sometimes ran along the ridge of a hill so that from the cockpit of our boat we had a glorious view of the rolling countryside below.

As for the towns themselves - again, another world, though far from beautiful. Here the water was often filthy and evil-smelling, with old motor tyres, bicycle frames and bedsteads threatening to damage our propeller. Dead dogs and cats would bump against the side

---

Fig. 5.2 *Specimen layout of the first page of an article or short story*

name and address. (The title sheet is removed and sent to the Accounts Department if your MS is accepted, hence the need for the duplicated information.) A quarter of the way down the page, type the title and the by-line once again, leave a double-double space, indent your five spaces and begin your article or story. Your name or the title should appear at the top of every page in case the sheets come adrift, and it is a good idea to repeat your name and address on the last page of the MS.

Be sure that your typewriter ribbon is not in need of replacement. Some time ago I was judging a short story competition set by a local Writers' Circle, and one entry was typed so faintly that I could hardly decipher it. I almost gave up in disgust but luckily I didn't; that story was the winner! An editorial office, with hundreds of manuscripts to deal with, would certainly return such a story unread.

When your manuscript is ready, fasten the pages together with a slide-on clip. On no account fold the manuscript more than once (it is really best to pack your work flat). Always enclose a stamped, self-addressed envelope of the right size, but there is no need to send a covering letter unless you have a special reason to do so (e.g. you have some good colour transparencies to illustrate your article; you have run a stamp shop for the past ten years, hence your authority for writing an article on new trends in philately). Keep your letter very brief and don't mention any personal matter unless it is strictly related to the article. Short stories seldom require a letter. Articles should be addressed to the Features Editor and short stories to the Fiction Editor if the periodical uses both types of material. Otherwise just send your MS to the Editor.

You must never send the same piece to two markets at the same time. This is totally unethical and your name will be black-listed if you do so. Allow at least two months for a reply. If you receive no news in that time, write politely to ask if they have reached a decision. On no account request a personal interview; your work must speak for itself.

By the time your MS has been to several journals it will begin to look untidy. Don't begrudge the time for retyping. In any case you will probably need to rewrite it to suit a different market, but never submit a typescript which is anything but clean and neat. Creased pages, tea stains (editors are great tea and coffee drinkers) or curled-up corners will ruin your chances. A protective extra sheet of paper at the back can often save you work and creases may respond to an iron, but there is often nothing for it but to grit your teeth and sit down to a stint of retyping. We all hate it but it's an essential part of the writer's craft and must be done with as good a grace as we can muster. By the way, be sure you don't send out a manuscript with the last rejection slip still attached. It *has* been done!

Finally, it is advisable to keep a special notebook to record the comings and goings of your manuscripts. The book can be ruled into columns with 'Title; Where Sent; Date Sent; Date Returned; Remarks; Fee Paid'. It's a great day when you first fill in that right-hand column! It isn't just the cheque that delights you – it's the knowledge that an editor is prepared to buy your work. He thinks it is well-written and that his readers will enjoy it. All your efforts have been worthwhile.

Exercise 5

Type out Exercise 2, following the instructions for submitting an article.

6

The Short Story

Nothing is wasted

It is very easy to write a bad short story; I know from bitter experience. The ones I wrote as a beginner are there to remind me – a drawer full of discoloured old quarto manuscripts held together with rusty paper clips. But although short stories require a different technique from novels, I realise now that those early failures were a necessary apprenticeship. It was through the years of writing and rewriting – struggling to express myself clearly, to work out my plots, to bring the characters to life – that I learned the skills I needed to produce a full-length novel. None of our writing is wasted. There will be days when you feel that you haven't produced a single sentence to your satisfaction, but we all have those days and they are necessary to our development. Eventually we discover the form of writing we are best at – long or short, fiction or non-fiction, for children or for adults – but until we find that out, *all* our writing is valuable experience. Don't throw anything away! You never know when you may need odd paragraphs for reference or to include in some later story. I learnt my lesson when I had to empty the dustbin to retrieve a torn and crumpled page from the garbage.

Short stories can be any length from 800 to 7000 words, depending on the market, but 2250 is a good length for a 'practice' story as it fits the fifteen-minute radio slot.

You may be wondering what was wrong with those early efforts of mine. Some were too macabre, too melodramatic;

beginners often find themselves drawn to write of suffering and violence, possibly because it is easier to create a dramatic effect in this way, and also, of course, to relieve their private griefs. (Never let us overlook or denigrate ·the therapeutic value of creative writing; getting our sorrows down on paper, disguised and reconstructed into fiction, can go a very long way towards removing them.) Some of my stories were nothing more than a series of loosely related incidents based on my schooldays or on my war years in the Air Force; they weren't short stories at all. Others were too long-winded, full of poetic phrases which I used to think of as 'fine writing'. They were all quite unsaleable but I kept on sending them out and collecting rejection slips. Sometimes I had a letter to say that my work 'showed promise', but nobody told me what was wrong with it. Regrettably, editors haven't time for that.

It wasn't until I joined a Writers' Circle that I began to see my mistakes and find out what really went into the making of a good short story. Of course, like most people who want to write them, I had read a great many, but reading for enjoyment is not enough; one must dissect, analyse, ask oneself questions. How did he open the story? How and when was the main character introduced? What gave life to the setting? And what made the story *move*?

In the preface to his book *The Modern Short Story*, H. E. Bates says that '*it is the most difficult and exacting of all prose forms*'. This is generally accepted to be the case, and yet it is the form most commonly attempted by the beginner – and rightly so, because here he will be able to test his skills and learn his trade. He will learn the art of writing concisely, the swift but telling portrayal of character, the steady development towards a satisfying climax.

How, then, as a novice, are you to find the way to success? Here are the ingredients, as I see them, for a short story which will be not only a joy to write but a saleable commodity when it is completed. Let's assume, to begin with, that you have a lively imagination and the ability to write grammatical prose; without these qualifications, short story writing is not for you. We will discuss the so-called 'straight' short story; fantasies, science fiction, children's stories and formula romances demand their own particular techniques, although most of the guidelines still apply.

The ingredients

1　An original idea

It is true that hackneyed, uninspiring stories, if competently written, do appear in print but it seems to me that they are of little value to the reader and can't have given the writer a great deal of satisfaction. (The satisfaction of cashing the cheque? Yes, but how much greater the satisfaction *and* the cheque might be if the story had real quality.)

Your idea may come to you 'out of the blue', a sudden inspiration while you sit in a train, wash the dishes or lie awake at night. On the other hand it may be sparked off by something that has happened to you, or by something you saw on television or read in a newspaper. Whatever it is, *it must excite you*. It must set you tingling with eagerness to get it down on paper. This idea is your theme. It answers the question you should always ask yourself before you begin any piece of writing: 'What am I trying to *say*?' The events in your story (the plot), however interesting or dramatic, must also have significance. Even a light-hearted tale should reveal something important about human relationships.

2　Believable characters

Character, of course, is at the heart of all fiction (see Chapters 9 and 10). A short story revolves around one central character whose problem will become of increasing interest. The reader must be made to feel at the outset that he knows and cares about this person, and you can best bring this about by the use of a single viewpoint throughout the story – that is, *seeing everything through that one person's eyes*. I believe that it is vital to stay in the mind of your central character from the first word to the last. Stories are published which ignore this rule, but when you are a beginner you should adhere to it very strictly. Later you may occasionally decide to change viewpoint in order to create a special effect, but you will understand exactly what you are doing and why you are doing it. Be sure to choose the right central character. Ask yourself, before you plan your story: 'Whose problem is it?' If in doubt, choose the character with whom you sympathise. Unless *you* care, your readers will not care.

First person or third? This is always a difficult decision; it depends on the story and on your own individual approach to the theme and the situation. The first person is probably easier to write, as one can identify more readily with an 'I' character, and emotions can be expressed more naturally. And of course there are no viewpoint problems.

Dialogue is essential: people reveal themselves by the things they say, and the reader, hearing the voices of your characters, will feel that he knows them. '*He often spoke unkindly to his wife*' is far less effective than a scene in which you show the two of them together and let us hear exactly what he says to her and in what circumstances. In other words, choose direct narrative whenever possible, painting a vivid picture of a particular occasion, rather than making generalisations.

Although you will have to bring your characters to life in a few words, you need not deny yourself the luxury of the memorable phrase, the original observation. Descriptions can be concise yet richly evocative; this is a part of your craft.

3 A convincing background
Your characters should move in a realistic setting, briefly evoked like the characters themselves. Atmosphere is of great importance. You must take the reader into an imaginary world, make him believe in it, and do so *at once* (see Chapter 11).

You would be wise to choose the kind of setting you know; not necessarily a real place, of course, but somewhere you can picture in your mind's eye without difficulty. Lighting is important, and movement – a sudden flash of sunlight on a water jug, the shadow of a man across a cobbled street, the swaying of willow branches reflected in water. You can only bring these things to life for the reader if you can see them with the inner eye of your imagination.

Pay attention to sounds and smells, as well as the way

things look. Fiction-writing demands the use of all our senses.

4   A good opening

You should introduce your main character without delay, expressing his *feelings* and avoiding long descriptions and explanations. There is probably something wrong with your story if, by the bottom of page 2, you have failed to introduce your main character, state his/her problem and establish an intriguing situation. I attach great importance to the first two pages. Here you must arouse your reader's curiosity or run the risk of losing him for ever. It's no use having a brilliant scene on page 4 if nobody gets that far!

5   Conflict

No short story can exist without conflict. Your central character must be faced with a problem at the outset; it may be in the shape of a person, a decision, ambition, dread, the forces of nature or of war, but no story will hold the reader's attention unless there is some kind of early confrontation. Contented people are hopelessly unsuitable material for fiction; sadly, there is no drama in peace and happiness!

6   Suspense

Suspense and plot are closely connected. Having set the scene with your main character in a situation of conflict, your object is to maintain momentum until the end. Readability, an essential quality in any kind of writing, depends on beguiling the reader into turning the page; this means that the interest must never flag, that you must stick to the main story line and build up inexorably to the final climax. This by no means implies that your story must be packed with dangerous dilemmas and breathless drama. A delicate atmospheric story can be equally enthralling if you build up the tension in the mind of your viewpoint character. A state of anxiety, if we care about the person, can provide unbearable suspense. (Does he love her? How will so-and-so react? When will the telephone ring?) With practice you will learn to think in terms of dramatic situations, discarding the trivial and the tedious, and commanding the reader's unswerving attention. If you are worried about 'plotting' you will find it helpful to build on the first dramatic situation. Every scene will suggest another scene; it's as if each confrontation lights an explosive charge which ignites the next one. You might be able to plan the whole story before you begin – and it's advisable, if you can – but many writers develop the action as they go along, finding inspiration in the dilemmas of their characters. Suspense, whether subtle and low-key or of great intensity, is the very life-blood of successful fiction. You are inventing a piece of life, but unlike real life, your story must have an artistic form, a framework to hold it tightly together. And this brings us to the next ingredient.

7 Shape

Quite simply, this means a Beginning, a Middle and an End. There is no substitute for sound construction, although you may choose to develop your story along unconventional lines.

Basically, the Beginning introduces the characters, sets the scene and poses the problem; the Middle develops the action and involves the reader in a situation of increasing fascination; the End resolves the problem, for better or worse. Be sure that everything is relevant to your theme. Be ruthless in pruning away all superfluous incidents, descriptions, even characters. And keep your time span fairly short, avoiding spaces to denote the passage of weeks or months. A single problem and a single period of time will give your story that tautness of construction which is so important. Once you have brought it to a conclusion, don't extend it into anti-climax with needless explanations. Let it speak for itself.

8 A satisfying ending

The ending need not be a happy one. It's enough for us to nod our heads, wisely and sadly, saying to ourselves, 'Yes, that's life!' A totally happy ending is seldom satisfying to the discerning reader because it is not convincing; life doesn't work like that. The best endings are unexpected but inevitable, so that we look up from the final word and gasp 'Of course!' Some stories leave us thinking 'Oh, *no*!' (the contrived) or 'So what?' (the banal). I like a note of hope in my short story endings, as I do with plays and novels – the feeling that the main character has been through some difficult times but has emerged in a better position to face the future. Am I saying, then, that your hero or heroine should not be permitted to die? Yes, I think I am. The death of the hero, with whom the reader has identified, comes like a little death for him as well. And there is another point. You may have heard the anecdote about a man who nodded off to sleep in a chair and dreamed he was an aristocrat in the French Revolution with his head on the block waiting for the guillotine to descend. Someone tapped him on the back of the neck with a book at the precise moment when the blade fell, and the shock caused the man to die in his sleep.

Aha, but in that case, how could anyone have known about the dream? The same problem arises if you allow your viewpoint character to die. The art of fiction is a strange deceit; the author tells us lies as if they were true, and yet there is a kind of integrity behind the make-believe, a sense of what is acceptable and what is not.

Twenty common faults

Theme too ordinary
The wrong central character
Slow beginning
Too many characters
Shallow characterisation
Change of viewpoint
Time span too long
Contrived situations
Too much trivia
Too much poetic imagery

Lack of clarity
Lack of shape
Lack of conflict
Too little dialogue
Stilted dialogue
Irrelevant episodes
Slip-shod writing
Too much generalisation
Flat ending
Cheat ending (e.g. it was a dream)

Some classic openings

The following openings demonstrate how the authors have launched the story, created an atmosphere and introduced the main character at the same time. When you have learned to intermingle characterisation, setting and action, you have mastered one of the most important techniques of fiction writing.

'Down below there was only a vast white undulating sea of cloud. Above there was the sun, and the sun was white like the clouds, because it is never yellow when one looks at it from high in the air.

He was still flying the Spitfire. His right hand was on the stick and he was working the rudder-bar with his left leg alone. It was quite easy. The machine was flying well. He knew what he was doing.

Everything is fine, he thought. I'm doing all right. I'm doing nicely. I know my way home. I'll be there in half an hour. When I land I shall taxi in and switch off my engine and I shall say, help me to get out, will you. I shall make my voice sound ordinary and natural and none of them will take any notice. Then I shall say, someone help me to get out. I can't do it alone because I've lost one of my legs. They'll all laugh and think I'm joking and I shall say, all right, come and have a look, you unbelieving bastards. Then Yorky will climb up on to the wing and look inside. He'll probably be sick because of all the blood and the mess. I shall laugh and say, for God's sake, help me get out.'

(*Beware of the Dog* by Roald Dahl)

'Mr Penfold, a travelling draper and haberdasher, easy terms arranged, a painfully shy, retreating man with almost invisible eyelashes, who looked as if he would have been much happier walking backwards, struggled out into the countryside every other Thursday on a massive basket-work tricycle, and called on Mrs Armitage, a war-widow, and her daughter Katie. Mr Penfold, who was in his early forties, was a single man.'

(*Mr Penfold* by H. E. Bates)

'The telephone rang beside the bed in the middle of the night and she woke struggling across her husband's body to grab the receiver. Their movements under the bedclothes might have denoted mating or fighting; the fact was that even in sleep she was alert to the humiliation of hearing him answer the telephone without teeth in his mouth.'

(*A Mad One* by Nadine Gordimer)

'He simply said my name. He said "Martha", and once again I could feel it happening. My legs trembled under the big white cloth and my head became fuzzy, though I was not drunk. It's how I fall in love. He sat opposite. The love object. Elderly. Blue eyes. Khaki hair.'

(*The Love Object* by Edna O'Brien)

The following quotation from Nadine Gordimer's introductions to her own *Selected Stories* will give you a foretaste of the possibilities which await you when you begin this beguiling task. '*A short story* occurs *in the imagination. To write one is to express from a situation in the exterior or interior world the life-giving drop – sweat, tear, semen, saliva – that will spread in intensity on the page; burn a hole in it.*' (Note her delightful use of the word 'express'.)

Exercise 6

Choose a theme and central character for a short story. Make notes for a Beginning, Middle and End, and write the first two pages. (Your Exercise 1 may provide a basis.)

7

The Radio Story

A short story designed for radio is basically the same as that for the printed page but there are some important points to bear in mind. A story which is to be read over the air must, like a radio talk, be written in an easy conversational style, avoiding long words, long sentences and literary phrases, although the writing can – and should – be alive with imagery.

Characterisation is of the greatest importance. The story should revolve around one person's problem and a single period of time. Jumps of several days or weeks are usually unsatisfactory in a fifteen-minute story (which is in fact fourteen-and-a-half minutes to allow for the announcement of the title, your name and the name of the reader). The length required is about 2250 words, and you must remember that the first minute is decisive. The listener will either switch off or settle down to enjoy himself, depending on those vital 150 words.

Take these two openings:

1 'Whenever I see a green sports car I feel an overwhelming desire to smash the windscreen. It's all because of Molly Shipton, who won the village beauty contest last summer.'

2 'One morning in late autumn I was standing alone on the platform of a country station in Wiltshire. I had five minutes to wait before my train came in and I occupied myself by counting the pigeons on the roof of a nearby house. It was a

cold day and as I stamped my feet to keep warm, the pigeons took flight, their sudden movement the only stir in the still, frosty air.'

Most people would have tuned to another station or switched off the set by the end of example 2. Example 1, I think, is sufficiently promising to make the listener stay with it. Sports cars and beauty queens have high interest value. Country stations and rows of pigeons have none unless there is some other factor to indicate an intriguing development. 'Ah,' says the author, 'but there *is* an intriguing development when the train comes in.' 'What?', I ask, 'Five minutes later?' The solution, of course, is to start the story when the train comes in, to begin when the kettle is beginning to boil, not when it is filled at the tap.

The first person singular is particularly appropriate for a radio story as it gives the impression of someone confiding a personal experience. Don't introduce too many characters – not more than four, I would suggest – and be sure that your writing is intensely visual. Listeners often have their eyes closed and you have a fine opportunity to create colourful impressions (e.g. 'The pillar box was a blinding scarlet in the sunlight').

Remember that fictitious dialogue is more, much more, than mere conversation. Every word must count (see Chapter 10). Don't include a single exchange which does not advance the story or deepen the characterisation – preferably *both at the same time*.

According to *Writing for the BBC 'there is a preference for strong plots rather than impressionistic writing'*. It is important to avoid generalisations such as 'Shop assistants can be very unfriendly'. Instead you might say: 'The woman behind the counter stared at Kay as if she had no right to be in the shop.' Genuine issues of the day provide good subjects – street violence, loneliness, redundancy, the generation gap and so on, but a sombre theme, as you will hear again when we consider The Novel (Chapter 16), need not mean that the story is depressing. The courage and imagination people show in the face of trouble is always an inspiration. As with the magazine story, try to make your ending both unexpected and inevitable. Keep to a single viewpoint, seeing the situation only through the eyes of your central character. Other characters will speak and react, but we shall not know their thoughts; the listener must identify with your chosen protagonist from the beginning to the end. This advice holds good for any story, but for radio it is particularly important.

If your story has a regional flavour – say, a drama set in a Welsh mining village – send it first to the appropriate region. If it is rejected there, you can still submit it to London, but not *vice versa*. (Don't ask me why!)

Unlike the radio talk, stories are seldom read by their authors (though you can apply to do so if you wish). Professional actors and actresses are usually employed as readers, and you can be sure that your work will have excellent presentation.

Listen to as many broadcast stories as possible – and not only those you enjoy. Write down the qualities that please and displease you, learning continually how to make the most of this unique and challenging medium.

Exercise 7

Write the first three minutes of a radio story (about 450 words).

8

The Practical Approach

The more you read, the more easily you can distinguish between good writing and bad, but when you become a writer and find yourself face to face with a blank sheet of paper, it is very difficult to express your ideas in the way you would like. Nor is it easy to know how well or how badly you are doing. You're too close to it; it's hard to be objective.

Getting started

Let's imagine you have an idea that pleases you and feel you are ready to write the first sentence. Everyone has his own way of working and you will develop the method that suits you best, but here are some suggestions for getting started.

First of all, think about your idea very carefully and ask yourself that vital question: 'What am I trying to *say*?' Whatever branch of writing you attempt, that same question is always relevant.

The next thing is to decide which medium is the most appropriate. Perhaps you have chosen the short story when a radio play might be a better vehicle for your idea. On the other hand there might not be enough body in your theme to warrant either of these; maybe you could express it more effectively in a poem. Sometimes you can only discover the right medium by trial and error.

When you have come to a decision, prepare some notes for a possible Beginning, Middle and End. A certain amount of planning is always necessary but some people require more than others. When I ask my students to write down their main problems, the same two always head the list: How to start, and How to get shape into your work. They are closely related because the shape must be part of the original plan, even though it may require adjustment – or even radical change – as you go along. The argument against writing a story or an article straight off in a wild rush of enthusiasm is that the lack of planning is pretty sure to be apparent unless you are highly skilled. Thus you will find that you have put unnecessary work into something which could have been improved by more initial thought.

Revision

Some writers feel the need to perfect each sentence as far as possible before going on to the next; I work that way myself. Others prefer to rough the whole thing out in full and then go back and revise it. In any case, your work will be subject to constant revision right to the final draft, so don't be discouraged if you have to cross things out and scribble alterations between the lines and up the sides and on spare bits of paper. My working pages are still festooned with arrows and asterisks, and as soon as I have typed out a fair copy from my longhand muddle, I find myself scrawling amendments all over it again. Take a look at my last corrected draft of the Introduction to this book (Fig. 8.1).

I think it unwise, especially in fiction, to prepare a rigid plan and force yourself to stick to it. Every piece of writing should remain fluid, open to new and unexpected developments which flower from your original idea as you work. Nicholas Monsarrat, who wrote *The Cruel Sea*, said in a letter to a novice: '*Never wait for inspiration. Sit down at the typewriter or notebook and get to work. Get something down on paper every day, and take a look at it next morning, and see how you can improve it. There is not a paragraph in the world which cannot be improved by rephrasing.*' This is perhaps an exaggeration but you will find that every sentence you write requires more thought than you ever anticipated. Here is an example of the way in which I battled with a sentence to make it more concise, more telling. I was describing a night journey by train.

(*a*)   Lighted stations flung themselves for an instant against the window and then were sucked away into the blackness.

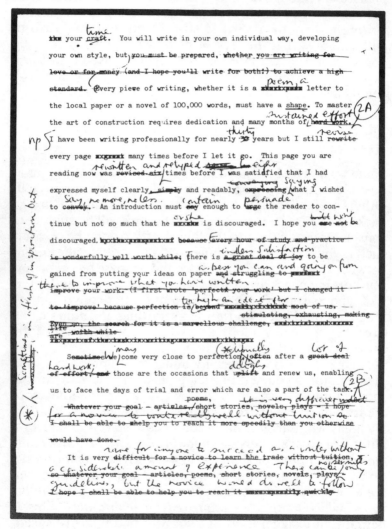

Fig. 8.1   *Final draft of part of my Introduction, before retyping*

(*b*)   Small lighted stations flared against the window from time to time and then were sucked away into the blackness.
(*c*)   Little lighted stations flared against the window from time to time and were instantly sucked into the blackness.
(*d*)   Little stations flared against the window from time to time and were instantly sucked away into the darkness.

Perhaps you are thinking that one can go on too long with such amendments, draining the life from your prose. There is always the danger of over-correction but the novice is much more likely to err the other way, and in any case the practice of improvement is an essential part of your training as a writer.

Don't you agree, in version (*c*), that 'lighted' is unnecessary? The station would hardly 'flare' if it were not lighted! And 'darkness', following 'into the' has a smoother sound than 'blackness'. Euphony is of great importance; that's why you should always read your work aloud, preferably onto a tape recorder so that you can check the manuscript as you listen to the playback.

When you start the actual writing, it is a good idea to stop at the end of the first page and ask yourself the following questions:

1   Has the opening sentence sufficient impact?
2   Have I started at the right point?
3   Is this page interesting enough to make the reader want to continue?
4   Have I written it clearly and simply?
5   Have I arranged my material in the right order?
6   Is everything strictly relevant to my theme?

Pause at the end of every page, or even every paragraph, and question yourself along these lines. When you reach the end of the whole piece, read it through from beginning to end with great care, checking for repetitions, clumsy phrases, clichés and so on (see Chapter 12). If a sentence or phrase refuses to be reworded satisfactorily, I have sometimes found that the solution lies in deleting it altogether. Not so with the previous sentence! It contains useful advice and I had to rewrite it seven times before I was satisfied. The six discarded versions were as follows:

(*a*)   If a phrase refuses to be reshaped despite many attempts, the answer may be to delete it altogether.

(*b*)   If a sentence or phrase presents constant difficulty I have found that it can sometimes be deleted altogether.

(*c*)   If a sentence or phrase refuses to satisfy you despite many attempts, the answer may be to delete it altogether.

(*d*)   If a sentence or phrase presents endless difficulty I have often found that the solution lies in deleting it altogether.

(*e*)   If a sentence or phrase persistently refuses to satisfy you, the solution may lie in deleting it altogether.

(*f*)   If a sentence or phrase refuses to be reworded satisfactorily, I have often found that the solution lies in deleting it altogether.

Note that in the final version I replaced 'often' with 'sometimes' because in fact it doesn't happen very frequently.

There is a tendency for the beginner to avoid facing up to his mistakes because of all the work which correcting them will entail. Successful writers never hesitate to correct a fault because it is too much trouble to put it right; that's one of the reasons why they are successful.

What, then, are the main qualities which any piece of writing should possess if it is to satisfy the reader? The following five are at the top of my list: *interest*, *liveliness*, *shape*, *clarity* and *style*. You may find it rewarding to list any others which seem to you important.

Exercise 8

Rewrite your article along the lines suggested, type it out again and send it to your chosen market.

9

Characterisation

Creating believable characters

'To write fiction,' said Aldous Huxley, *'one needs a whole series of inspirations about people in an environment, and then a whole lot of hard work on the basis of those inspirations.'* Your characters must come to life as full-blooded individuals with strong emotions, authentic talk and convincing reactions to every situation if your work is to satisfy the reader. In order to create such characters you must get to know them very well indeed. This means thinking about them deeply, searching out their secret fears and longings, standing back from them without judging, yet also, paradoxically, identifying with them even though they are quite different from yourself.

To introduce oneself into a short story or a novel is, in my view, a great mistake. This would be a kind of autobiography, not fiction. *'A good novel tells us the truth about its hero but a bad novel tells us the truth about its author'* (from *Heretics* by G. K. Chesterton). It is unsatisfactory (as well as potentially libellous!) to represent people from real life. Fiction is imaginary; it may be sparked off by actual people and actual events but the author should be inventing characters and situations to illustrate his theme; when he creates the characters himself he understands their background, their motives and every turn of thought. How can we possibly know a real person in such depth? No one reveals his deepest secrets; there is always something he would never divulge to anyone. That 'something', known to you about your imaginary hero, is often the mainspring of the story.

Your characters may, of course, be *based* on people you have met, probably an amalgam of many. They will almost certainly include aspects of yourself, the person you understand the best, but you will be creating an individual who has never existed before. What a challenge!

I love this quotation from Pirandello: '*When the characters are really alive before their author, the latter does nothing but follow them in their action, in their words, in the situation which they suggest to him*' (from *Six Characters in Search of an Author*). If you write a novel you will probably find that the plot is suggested by the characters, almost as if they were acting out the story for themselves as the book progresses; it's like a film unrolling in front of your eyes. Sometimes the film breaks down and this is when your characters can help you out. Pay attention to their needs and they will restore the continuity.

Your central figure should be someone for whom you, as the author, can feel affection. He may have faults and weaknesses but he should not, I think, be shallow or cowardly or cruel. There is a case for the anti-hero and we may sometimes enjoy reading about a villain to see if he gets his deserts, but in general the novice would be wise to choose a protagonist with whom he can readily sympathise.

If you are writing a who-dun-it, a thriller or a science-fiction story you may feel that plot and suspense are more important than the participants. In some ways this is true, but good characterisation can only enhance any work of fiction and you would be well advised to study it carefully, whatever genre you eventually decide upon.

Choosing names

It is difficult to envisage a character until you have found the perfect name. Names are of great importance – nicknames, too – and you should never make do with something that does not satisfy you. Somehow you will know if it isn't quite right; listen to that inner voice and be guided by your intuition, your sense of good judgment or whatever you prefer to call it.

Be sure that your names are not too similar: for example, Claudia and Laura, Karen and Marion, Nigel and Simon. Contrast is important when you are choosing your cast. In the same way, make your forenames and surnames complement one another. Dominic Smith is good; Dominic Fotheringay is bad. Two flamboyant names together lack conviction. There's no harm in using the telephone book for ideas. Open a page at random and the gods may deliver the very surname you want.

How much description

In the old days it was customary to describe people in great detail; several pages were devoted to one character. Contemporary readers would seldom have the time or inclination to dally so long. They like to use their own imagination, building on the author's brief but telling phrases. Study this description of Cordelia in *An Unsuitable Job for a Woman* by P. D. James:

> 'Between their shoulders she could see her own reflection in the mirror above the bar. Today's face looked no different from yesterday's face; thick, light brown hair framing features which looked as if a giant had placed a hand on her head and the other under her chin and gently squeezed the face together; large eyes, browny-green under a deep fringe of hair; wide cheek bones; a gentle, childish mouth. A cat's face she thought, but calmly decorative among the reflection of coloured bottles and all the bright glitter of Mavis's bar.'

You should also learn to weave your characterisation into the development of the story as Ian McEwan has done in this extract from his brilliant novel, *The Cement Garden*:

> 'That night my parents argued over the bags of cement. My mother, who was a quiet sort of person,

was furious. She wanted my father to send the whole lot back. We had just finished supper. While my mother talked my father used a penknife to scrape black shards from the bowl of his pipe on to the food he had barely touched. He knew how to use his pipe against her. She was telling him how little money we had and that Tom would soon be needing new clothes for starting at school. He replaced the pipe between his teeth like a missing section of his own anatomy and interrupted to say it was "out of the question" sending the bags back and that was the end of it.'

You will find that unusual detail is the most evocative. Everyone has some idiosyncrasy to distinguish him or her from the rest and you should search out these qualities in your characters.

'Her mother sat upright in the rickshaw with something of the appearance of a moulting hawk: a woman of nearly sixty whose face had the arid shantung-yellow texture that came of thirty years' service under the Burma sun. She wore a dress of dull brown silk that, from the acid of much sweat, had gone completely to pieces under the arms. It had been reprieved with parallelograms of lighter colour that would have shown badly if Mrs McNairn had ever lifted her arms more than waist high. In her determination to do no such thing she sat with her arms clenched in her lap, grasping the ivory handle of her white parasol. It was the parasol, with its hooked handle curving out from her clenched hands and knees, rather than anything in her angular beaky face, that gave the appearance of a faded bird of prey.'

(*The Jacaranda Tree* by H. E. Bates)

It is usually more effective to portray a person at a particular time and place in the story, as with the last two examples, rather than give a more general description.

At this point I should like to quote from an earlier book of mine called *The Craft of Novel-Writing* (Allison and Busby):

> 'Sometimes a character becomes so real that he refuses to do what you have planned for him. When this happens, don't coerce him; it means you have created a real person with a will of his own and this is a marvellous moment in any novelist's life. Hold him on a light rein, as it were, giving him his head to a certain degree but ensuring that he does not stampede you out of your story. You must remain in command whilst allowing your creations to behave in accordance with the qualities you have given them. Write your scene with all the skill you have and let your instinct tell you whether or not it carries conviction. Creating imaginary characters is the core of novel-writing – and the possibilities are endless.'

Bear in mind that your main character will undergo a change, subtle or violent, as a result of the various pressures he has faced. It may be the onset of bitterness or despair, a deepening of understanding, the effects – beneficial or otherwise – of falling in love, embracing some cause or belief, suffering an injury. In a short story the development of character is more difficult to express, but the novelist reveals the truth of his vision by the gradual change which takes place in his hero or heroine as the story unfolds; one of the signs of a 'cardboard' character is that he is exactly the same at the end of the book as he was at the beginning.

If the development is a change for the better, the novel will obviously be more satisfying to the reader, but there are no rules; you must write the way you feel, tell the truth for your characters, know them, and show them, and make the reader care about them.

Exercise 9

Write a character study of 500 words. If you intend to be a fiction-writer, choose an imaginary person.

10

Dialogue

'What is the use of a book,' thought Alice, *'without pictures and conversation?'* We all know how she felt; the conversation you introduce into your fiction is of paramount importance. In this chapter we will consider the dialogue in short stories and novels; for stage or television plays, where the characters are there in person, the approach is rather different, and radio drama demands a special technique of its own (see Chapter 18). No matter what type of fiction you are writing, the dialogue must sound as if real people are talking to each other, but fictional dialogue is very different from actual speech; the dull bits, the repetitions, the irrelevancies, must be pruned away, leaving a taut, interesting exchange which gives the *impression* of real speech.

A beginner once said to me, defending a page of tedious dialogue: 'But I heard two women saying all that in a bus shelter – I wrote it down in shorthand!' It's essential, of course, to listen (quite shamelessly) to conversations in queues and trains so that you are aware of the way in which many kinds of people speak to each other, but that is only background study. When you write the dialogue in your story you must be ruthless in cutting out every single word which does not carry the action forward or add something significant to the delineation of your characters. As you gain experience you will learn to incorporate both at the same time.

You might think that you must make the dialogue boring if you are to portray a boring person. Not so. If you show the reaction of someone else, someone who is far from boring, your tedious character will be revealed effectively and yet you will keep the reader interested – and possibly amused as well. (If you find yourself putting two bores together, replan the scene!)

The following examples show how a beginner's story can be improved by editing. As you become more accomplished you will edit as you go along – or afterwards, depending on your personal preference.

> 'Marion was standing by the living room door with her coat on.
>
> "I'll just have to pop down to the chemist's, John," she explained. "I've got to wash my hair tonight and I need some more shampoo. I didn't realise it was all used up and I can't use soap because it makes my hair look dull, even if I rinse it over and over again. I won't be long – only about twenty minutes – unless there's a queue in the shop. When I get back we'll talk about that horrible letter you got from your father."
>
> "Right," said John. "I'll do a bit of weeding while you're out."'

Boring, isn't it? It sounds like a real conversation, but for fiction it needs a great deal of pruning.

> 'Marion was standing by the living room door with her coat on.
>
> "I'm just going down to the chemist's for some shampoo," she said. "When I get back we'll talk about that letter."'

If John is going to do a bit of weeding while she's out, we don't want to know about it; he needs to get up to something much more intriguing. And the details of the letter can be omitted because it's apparent that the reader is already in the picture.

Good dialogue consists of lively speeches, usually short, in which people interrupt one another, deceive one another, go off at a tangent, sometimes use bad grammar and strong language, but never ramble on about nothing of importance, as we do in real life. Everything your characters say must be right for *them*. A novice will sometimes make two people speak in exactly the same way, even using the same expressions.

What about four-letter words? My own conviction is that we should allow our characters to use them (though not to excess) if it is appropriate for them to do so. An army sergeant would hardly say 'Go away!' if he found a man making love to his wife! If you dislike bad language this doesn't mean that you can't introduce it into your story; your characters will be doing plenty of things you disapprove of, besides swearing. But if you are so shocked by strong language that you can't write it (I once had a lady in my class who couldn't bring herself to say the word 'bloody' when she was reading out someone else's story) then you must choose the kind of characters who would not use the words you object to. My advice would be to write your dialogue truthfully (except in stories for children) but be prepared to bow to the editor's or publisher's wishes if he accepts your work and suggests amendments.

Avoid dialect as far as possible; it's difficult to read. A Yorkshire miner must obviously sound like a Yorkshire miner but his speech should be expressed by the turn of phrase rather than by apostrophes in place of letters. This will come easily if you are familiar with the kind of person you are writing about, and you should never choose to portray a section of the community which is not well known to you.

It is sometimes suggested that writers should search for alternatives to 'he said' and 'she said' (he demanded, she wavered, he expostulated, etc.). This is not only unnecessary but inadvisable. Study the masters of prose such as Graham Greene, H. E. Bates and Iris Murdoch, and you will find that 'said' is used a great deal and does not intrude in the least unless you are particularly looking out for it. Alternatives, deliberately sought for by amateurs, intrude all the time.

'"If Nicholas doesn't propose by the end of the month I shall ask him myself," exclaimed Jean.

"Oh, Jean – you can't!" protested Susan.

"I can and I will," affirmed Jean.

"If you do," continued Susan, "you'll lose him."

"I agree," averred Nigel . . .'

There are many occasions when no 'he said' is required, merely the speech itself, followed by the next one, but never allow confusion to arise by going on too long. If the reader has to count back to see who started you have failed as a writer.

Beware of the stilted phrase: *'I have told you that I did not do it'* instead of *'I've told you I didn't do it.'* Be sure to read your dialogue aloud; this is by far the best way to discover faults.

Novices often write their speeches in a vacuum. You should set your scene with great clarity so that we can picture your characters as they are speaking. I once had a student who wrote a marvellous exchange between two business-men, wrangling for power. It was dramatic and well edited but it failed because there was no background for their confrontation. They began in a car, driving through a leafy, sun-dappled lane, but as the dialogue continued there was no more mention of the environment. After a page or two we forgot they were in a car and when at last they got out of it we were flabbergasted.

You can often indicate who is speaking, by a verb of action rather than of speech, and this will help to give a visual image of the scene. For instance, *'I think I'm going to cry.'* Myra turned her head away. Or, *Eric tapped out his pipe and put it in his pocket. 'I've had enough – I'm going to bed.'*

For lay-out of dialogue on the page, study good contemporary writing and note that a new paragraph is required each time a different character speaks. Action by a character who has just spoken or who is about to speak, appears on the same line, as in the last two examples.

Single inverted commas are usually employed for dialogue, with double ones for quotes within a speech (e.g. 'I saw "The Three Sisters" at our local theatre last week.'), but publishers have their own preference and sometimes this procedure is reversed.

If thoughts are enclosed in inverted commas they can easily be confused with speech. My own technique is to begin the thought sequence with a capital letter: *She thought, He's no idea what I'm driving at.* You might prefer a colon to a comma after 'She thought'.

I am sometimes asked what proportion of dialogue should occur in a story or novel. This is a very difficult question but I would say, in general, not less than a third. A rough estimate would be one third dialogue, one third action and one third introspection, but it depends a great deal on the type of fiction. Dialogue is certainly essential to most stories and many writers find it the easiest part.

Exercise 10

Write 500 words of dialogue in which two people engage in a violent quarrel.

11

Setting

Your choice of setting should be one of the first considerations and be closely related to the theme, characters and action. Think carefully before you decide and make certain that you have chosen the most telling location for every scene you plan.

You will probably be influenced by places you have known quite briefly, places which have remained in your memory. Before I wrote my third novel, *Kick a Tin Can*, we had been living for a short time at Taplow, in Berkshire. Our home was a tiny flat and I was so excited by the beautiful riverside mansions that I invented one, a composite of several I had seen, enhanced by imagination, as the main setting for the novel. It was the story of an affair between a rich married woman of thirty-four and a boy of fifteen who lived in a slum.

'The Thames was quiet here, reflecting the dazzling facade of a large white house on the far bank. Wilfred imagined that a film star might live in such a place. There were conservatories, verandahs, a round tower with a shining gold weather-vane on the top, huge windows. A stone balustraded terrace, massed with pink geraniums, led to a long, well-kept lawn which sloped down to a landing stage and boathouse. The boathouse was empty, a cavern of mysterious green shadows and glimmers of refracted light. Beside it stood a weeping-willow tree and the lawn was surrounded by

yews and cedars ranging back, thick and dark, behind
the house itself, making its whiteness even more brilliant.'

I wrote that more than twenty years ago and now I think it
is too dense. The boathouse is essential because an important scene takes place there, but if I had the chance to rewrite
it I would relinquish the conservatories and verandahs.
Perhaps I would part with the tower as well, although I
would hate to do so; I can still see that weather-vane glinting
in the sunlight as clearly as if I were looking at a colour
transparency. And later in the book:

'He looked around him with more than his usual
disgust. What would Carol think, or Andrew, if they
could see the place where he lived? It was nothing but a
slum. Two rows of blackened little houses facing each
other across a narrow cobbled street. Grimy lace curtains in the tiny windows with sometimes a dusty plant
or a poor, miserable little budgie in a cage, to break the
monotony. Old cigarette packets and torn newspapers
in the gutters; dirty milk bottles in the doorways; the
smell of stale fat; cats and children exploring rubbish in
an alley-way; women in curlers shouting at them. . . .
He saw a curtain twitch as he passed a window and
caught the gleam of curious eyes on him.'

The main fault in that one, I think, is the repetition of the
word 'in'.
I created the two places, both imaginary but based on real
life, to highlight the contrast between the main characters.
A fictitious story may, of course, be set in an actual place,
so long as it is sufficiently large and impersonal. You can set
a novel in London, Chicago or Avignon, inventing street
names, hotels and bars, but you would be well advised not to
choose a small village which actually exists. You could
hardly use the one and only hotel as a background for your
drama; the manager might be very much put out, particularly if your story had a rather unsavoury theme! Small
places, therefore, should be totally imaginary, but a rough

idea of the location can be suggested by such phrases as 'hidden in a remote valley north of Lake Como' or 'just off the A33 between Winchester and Newbury'. Details of this kind give an illusion of reality but do not invite letters of complaint from your readers.

On pages 33 and 55 I have stressed the importance of seeing your background settings very clearly in your mind's eye. It is vital to picture your characters in a specific environment as they speak and move: the ability to see your story unreeling like a film is a skill you will need for fiction-writing and one which can be developed with practice if you have the basic gift.

Having captured your mental image, how are you to translate it into words? Study the following extract from a short story by Anton Tchekov entitled *Agafya: 'Beyond the hill the sun was setting. All that was left of the sunset was a pale crimson shaft of light, and even that was beginning to be overspread with flecks of cloud, as burning coal might be with ashes.'*

It's hard to believe, isn't it, that so striking a picture can be evoked by the use of such simple words and such a simple construction?

An unusual image sticks in the memory: the following scene from Margaret Drabble's *The Needle's Eye* will stay with me for ever because the picture of the hen is so quaint and delightful.

> 'They were in a waste lot, a steep bombed site: the house that adjoined the bombsite had appropriated a small plot of land, doubtless unofficially, and had fenced it off with wire, and in it were these hens. The wall that fronted on to the site still showed vestiges of the bombed building that had stood there: the remains of a fireplace one storey up, a few scraps of wallpaper. In the fenced-off plot stood an armchair. In the armchair sat a feathery dusty old hen.'

And how about this passage from *The French Lieutenant's Woman* by John Fowles, describing a woodland walk?

'It seemed strangely distinct, this undefiled dawn sun.
It had almost a smell, as of warm stone, a sharp dust of
photons streaming down through space. Each grass-
blade was pearled with vapour. On the slopes above his
path the trunks of the ashes and sycamores, a honey
gold in the oblique sunlight, erected their dewy green
vaults of young leaves; there was something myster-
iously religious about them, but of a religion before
religion; a druid balm, a green sweetness over all . . .'

I had to look up 'photons' (you too?) but that didn't
matter because the writing is so pure and exquisite.

Colour, movement, light and shade are all-important
when you visualise your scenes. You must know the time of
the year, the quality of light in every room and street and
garden you write about. You will not describe it all – how
could you? – but you must be aware of it if you are to give
the reader an acute sense of reality. Your characters should
move in a setting which is as true to life as they are themselves. This is often overlooked. A novice will describe the
sheen on a woman's hair, the colour and texture of her dress,
but not her shadow on the wall as the sun streams through
the window.

Your settings, of course, are not merely visual; we must
hear the traffic, the footsteps, the birdsong; we must smell
the appropriate smells – frying bacon, escaping gas, orange
blossom, anaesthetic. . . .

Write of what you know. Don't attempt to describe actual
locations you have never visited or to invent imaginary ones
with insufficient first-hand experience. You may argue that
some writers get away with it after extensive research but I
have always been against it. How can you hope to conjure up
the elusive sounds and smells of a country you have never
been to, or the particular atmosphere of an unknown town?
I pride myself on a healthy imagination but I wouldn't dream
of setting a book in Canada, for instance, until I had been
there. I could do it superficially perhaps but there would
be a myriad details I could never know about, and a native
would recognise their absence at once. If you have never
been to Venice, a football final, a bullfight, you would be

unwise to write about them; books and films cannot provide you with sufficient atmosphere. Historical settings, of course, can only be brought to life on the basis of research and guesswork, but at least there is no one around to tell us we are wrong – unless the occasional reader recalls a previous incarnation!

Describing imaginary places is one of the most satisfying aspects of a fiction-writer's job, so much so that he is apt to get carried away, introducing irrelevant details (like my conservatories and verandahs) and writing at too great a length. Limit yourself, in general, to no more than ten lines of description at a stretch, and make a habit of interspersing it with action.

> 'He pulled back the curtain a little and looked out into the November evening. Snow had begun to fall again in Ebury Street, large snow flakes moving densely, steadily, with visible silence, in the light of the street lamps, and crowding dimly above in the windless dark. A few cars hissed by, their sound muted and softened. The Count was about to say, 'It's snowing,' but checked himself. When someone is dying there is no point in telling him about the snow. There was no more weather for Guy.'
>
> (*Nuns and Soldiers* by Iris Murdoch)

Have you ever read a better description of snowfall? Looking up from the page, I was surprised to see a summer's day.

Exercise 11

Choose a house, real or imaginary, and bring it vividly to life in not more than 200 words.

12

Style

Your style is you

If you write in your own way you will gradually establish an individual style without conscious effort. I have been impressed, during many years of teaching Creative Writing, by the amazing variety in the work produced by complete beginners. After only a few meetings in which exercises are read out, the students recognise each other's work at once; the style is there, unique and unmistakable.

Although you should not attempt to copy anyone else's style, you can certainly learn from the writers you admire, study how they achieve their effects, and try to eliminate your own faults accordingly. For instance, in the chapter on Dialogue I pointed out that H. E. Bates used 'he said' and 'she said' far more than might be expected. This approach can be emulated without copying his style. Two of my favourite writers are Lawrence Durrell and Graham Greene. Their styles, as you may know, are totally different and I have learned from both and been inspired by them whilst in no way trying to mould my writing on theirs. Lawrence Durrell with his ornate literary turn of phrase has been accused of verbosity and this criticism might be justified if he were a lesser writer. Being the master he is, he can get away with it. Perhaps, in the course of time, you too might 'get away with it' but in the early stages I would suggest that you write clearly and simply, taking inspiration from Graham Greene rather than Lawrence Durrell. Wordy prose, over-complex and over-poetic, is certainly to be avoided. In a beginner this very fault may indicate a writer of great potential, but he must learn his trade and bear in mind that a direct contemporary style will find greater favour with editors and publishers.

Your particular approach may be pithy and pungent or leisurely and elegant; you should never, in your search for style, lose sight of a natural tendency. Always be consistent in your writing. For instance, if you start an article in a humorous vein you should maintain the humour to the end. It may seem obvious that a horror story should not change into a romance half way through and that a solid, informative reference book must not digress into a string of light-hearted anecdotes, but mistakes of this kind are often made.

It may seem that the pruning you have to do as a beginner will remove all trace of individuality from your work, leaving only a skeleton of that original concept which excited you so much. Don't be discouraged; one of the greatest problems any writer has to overcome is that of preserving spontaneity whilst honing away irrelevancies, repetitions and clumsy phrases. It *can* be done and it has to be done. Just give yourself time.

The enemies of good style

1 Incorrect grammar and punctuation
If you feel inadequate in these respects you should take a course, study *Fowler's Modern English Usage* or *The Elements of Style* by Strunk and White, and read as much good prose as you can, analysing it carefully to pinpoint your own mistakes. Small slips of grammar can be corrected by an editor or publisher but serious faults will spoil your chances of success.

It is outside the scope of this book to discuss punctuation in detail but I would urge you to study in particular the use of colons and semicolons and to limit the use of the exclamation mark; my own letters to friends are peppered with them but I have learned to restrict their use to the minimum in my novels.

Bad spelling is a much less serious problem than bad grammar. Here the words mean what you intend them to mean (we hope!) and are easily corrected; bad grammar can wreck whole paragraphs. Check your spelling with a dictionary whenever you are uncertain and learn the correct version as rigorously as if you were studying a new language.

2   Clichés

A cliché is defined by Fowler as 'a stereotype'. He goes on to say that *'in its literary sense it is a word or phrase whose felicity in a particular context when it was first employed has won it such popularity that it is apt to be used unsuitably or indiscriminately'*. Examples given include: filthy lucre; sleep the sleep of the just; tender mercies; leave no stone unturned. I could add to those, and so could you. How about silvery moonlight; heart-shaped face; pangs of remorse; knuckles standing out white; bouncing baby? If I went on to say that 'at this point in time' is one of my pet hates, you would probably exclaim: 'But "pet hate" is a cliché!' So it is, but I am writing this book in a rather conversational style and if I were to question every phrase, the prose would become too formal. Some people, in my view, are too strict about it; there are certain occasions when your exact meaning can be expressed in no other way. (Read what *Fowler's* has to say; it's fascinating.)

Beware of cliché *situations*: the woman who drops a glass when she hears some bad news; the husband who arrives home unexpectedly to find his wife in the arms of another man; the suicide note on the mantelpiece. Good style has a lot to do with freshness of vision.

3   Sentimentality

There is a world of difference between sentimentality and sentiment. Sentiment is sincere emotion – compassion, sorrow, love, delight. Sentimentality is mawkish, treacly, tearjerking, and according to the *Shorter Oxford Dictionary 'an exaggerated insistence upon the claims of sentiment'*. Your own good taste will tell you the difference, but the distinction can sometimes be a tricky one.

4 Clumsy phrases

The euphony of a sentence has a strong bearing on style. The writing may be correct grammatically but have a hard, jerky sound, leaving the reader with a sense of irritation rather than pleasure. For instance, 'every room and garden and street' is less harmonious than 'every room and street and garden'. Reading aloud will help, and if you stumble over a phrase, this may indicate that it needs revision. Your writing should run smoothly and easily, except on the rare occasions when you might choose an eccentric construction to obtain a certain effect. Take this example from *The War Lover* by John Hersey:

> 'Each of Buzz's landings was an experiment, a delicate search for a new and better way to find that breathtaking split moment when all those tons of metal ceased being carried by the wind and were accepted back by the mother ground. He held the wheel of the column in his fingertips and seemed to be feeling, with the sensitivity of a blind man reading Braille, for the very very very end of flight.'

Three very's in a row would normally be considered clumsy but in this instance I think they have been used with extraordinary courage and artistry.

Most of us can take any page of our work and improve it immensely by the removal of what I call 'dead wood'. These are words or phrases which are unnecessary, adding nothing but tedium. Here are some examples, with the 'dead wood' in italics: She crossed *over to the other side of* the road; they shared the *same* taxi; it was the first time they had *ever* quarrelled; he was *quite* sure that she meant to insult him. In the first draft of my earlier chapter on Dialogue I wrote the following passage:

> 'No matter what type of fiction you are writing, the dialogue must be convincing. This means that it must appear as if real people are talking to each other, but good dialogue in fiction is very different from actual speech; the dull bits, the irrelevancies, the needless

remarks we all include in our everyday conversation must be pruned away, leaving a taut, interesting exchange which gives the impression of real speech but is in fact nothing like it.'

I later reduced that rigmarole by a third:

'No matter what type of fiction you are writing, the dialogue must sound as if real people are talking to each other, but fictional dialogue is very different from actual speech; the dull bits, the repetitions, the irrelevancies, must be pruned away, leaving a taut, interesting exchange which gives the *impression* of real speech.'

You can imagine the forests of dead wood I have demolished since I began this book!

Anyone who went to school before the Second World War would do well to reconsider his English Grammar lessons. Many of us were taught that every sentence must contain a verb, that we must never begin a sentence with 'And' or end one with a preposition and so on. I suppose it was good basic training but it hampers some of my creative writing students. A sentence without a verb may puzzle you, but see how effective they can be: '*An empty room. No sound but a bluebottle at the window.*'

Be wary of adjectives

Most beginners love adjectives. It was years before I really understood that, far from enhancing descriptions, they can have a deadening effect. In order to point this out to my students I ask them to write a descriptive piece of 300 words *without the use of a single adjective*. It isn't easy but the results are an unfailing delight; some of the exercises are the best work the students have produced to date. When the pieces are finished, one adjective may be added, and the indulgence of this luxury makes it clear to everyone that adjectives should be chosen with infinite care.

The following 'no adjectives' exercise was written by a

beginner in a recent class. I quote it to allay your natural resistance to such a formidable task.

The Homecoming by Dorothy Wright:
'She turned the key in the lock, the door swung open and she stepped into the hall. Sunlight followed her in. She flicked the curtains at the window farther apart, and another shaft of light spread into the room. A mirror picked up the radiance, dust danced wherever the sun caught it.

The stairs stretched upwards on the left. She knew exactly what was in the cupboard underneath them – the vacuum cleaner, an assortment of boxes and a row of hooks bulging with coats. She recognised the ornaments on the shelf fixed over the radiator, the presents she and the others had brought back from holidays in Cornwall or on the Continent. Even the pictures greeted her like friends from childhood. The ticking of the clock standing in the corner caught her attention, and she saw that in ten minutes it would strike four o'clock.

But it was the table that drew her right inside. It stood in its place against the wall, the top shining from years of polishing. Its legs, and the stretchers joining them near their base, showing signs of maltreatment and damage in the past, but the carving on the drawer was as she remembered.

Two candlesticks stood on it, their metal twinkling. Between them on a mat was a bowl of flowers wearing fragrance like a halo. She moved closer, dropped her suitcase, and traced the carving on the drawer with her fingers, gently, lovingly, almost reverently. Then she leaned forward. With one hand she cupped a bloom and inhaled its sweetness. With the other she caressed the patina of the tabletop. It seemed to hold the warmth of life, and to welcome her home.'

For her one luxury adjective, the author chose the word 'delicate': '*the carving on the drawer was as delicate as she remembered.*' (You may be thinking that 'bulging', 'shining' and 'twinkling' are used as adjectives, but for the purpose of this exercise we mustn't be too pedantic.) The important thing is to aim high: trying for a difficult target usually produces quality, even if one falls a little short. In an exercise where adjectives are forbidden, the author will make compensatory use of adverbs. This adds liveliness to the piece but of course one must beware of using too many.

Once you have developed a good natural style you will never lose it. It will be there at your fingertips – a lasting pleasure for you yourself and for those who read your work.

Listen to Joseph Conrad:

> 'The attainment of proficiency, the pushing of your skill with attention to the most delicate shades of excellence, is a matter of vital concern. Efficiency of a practically flawless kind may be reached naturally in the struggle for bread. But there is something beyond – a higher point, a subtle and unmistakable touch of love and pride beyond mere skill; almost an inspiration, which gives to all work that finish which is almost art – which *is* art.'

> (*The Mirror of the Sea*)

The word 'bread', of course, has since acquired an ambiguity which catches our attention and may cause an inappropriate smile. This illustrates only too well the way in which language changes. Such changes cannot be ignored, however much they may sadden us; we must look ahead with zest, not backwards with nostalgia.

Exercise 12

Write a descriptive piece of 300 words or so, using no adjectives. When the work is finished, add one only.

13

Poetry

'There's no money in poetry,' someone complained to Robert Graves. 'No,' he replied, 'and there's no poetry in money!' It is by no means easy to sell a poem, but fortunately the need to express oneself in verse is usually an artistic and emotional need rather than a financial one. Children write poems for love alone and many adults do the same. People who contemplate the beauty of nature, long for freedom, worship God, or love one another in any of a thousand different ways, will often find they can express their feelings in poetry.

If you want to see your work in print, study the journals which publish verse and be sure to choose appropriate markets for your particular themes. You will stand a much better chance of getting a book of poems accepted by a publisher when you have achieved some success in magazines. The market for poetry is a very slender one, but if your work has special quality and you are not too easily discouraged, you may reach your goal.

How can you tell if your poems are good, bad or indifferent? That is a question I hesitate to answer. When we reflect that the work of some of the most distinguished contemporary poets is considered by some critics to be meaningless, we can understand how difficult it is to assess the true value of any poem. The ones you write with total sincerity might be condemned as 'gimmicky' or 'striving for effect'. A poem which was, in fact, composed with tongue in cheek may be acclaimed a masterpiece.

Poetry is such a personal thing; if it delights us, moves us deeply or opens new windows on life, then *for us* it has succeeded. Here are some lines from modern poets which have remained in my memory. Why not keep a notebook for your own selection?

'This lawn graced with the candle-flames of crocus'
      (from *A Happy View* by Cecil Day Lewis)

'There is a pike in the lake
whose blue teeth eat the midnight stars'
     (from *Juniper Holds to the Moon* by Laurie Lee)

'The force that drives the water through the rocks
Drives my red blood'
(from *The Force that Through the Green Fuse Drives the
          Flower* by Dylan Thomas)

'The night sky is only a sort of carbon paper,
Blueblack, with much-poked periods of stars
Letting in the light, peephole after peephole –
A bonewhite light, like death, behind all things.'
       (from *Insomniac* by Sylvia Plath)

'Take a black length of water, leave it rippling as the day
 dies,
By morning it will be stretched taut, pale and motionless,
 stiff silk.'
      (from *Cold Spell* by Vernon Scannell)

'What passing-bells for these who die as cattle?
Only the monstrous anger of the guns'
     (from *Anthem for Doomed Youth* by Wilfred Owen)

Construction

You will find it instructive to read the classics of poetry, old and new, and to study the imagery, the metre, the rhyme schemes, the overall design. You may prefer to discard conventional patterns – the choice between a traditional or a free form is a matter of personal taste – but some kind of shape is required no matter how unorthodox your verse may be. If you intend to specialise in this kind of creative writing you might study *The Poet's Manual* by Frances Stillman and the current *Poet's Yearbook*.

There is no better training than to compose a sonnet. The discipline of a set format is extremely valuable, whatever kind of verse you eventually choose to write.

Then hate me when thou wilt: if ever, now;
Now while the world is bent my deeds to cross,
Join with the spite of fortune, make me bow,
And do not drop in for an after-loss:
Ah, do not, when my heart hath scap'd this sorrow,
Come in the rearward of a conquer'd woe;
Give not a windy night a rainy morrow,
To linger out a purpos'd overthrow.
If thou wilt leave me, do not leave me last,
When other petty griefs have done their spite,
But in the onset come: so shall I taste
At first the very worst of fortune's might.

And other strains of woe, which now seem woe,
Compar'd with loss of thee, will seem not so.
            (*Sonnet Number XC* by William Shakespeare)

You will find that the best poems have a single theme – the inspirational idea – and that this central theme is expressed in a form which also has unity. Shakespeare's sonnets are prime examples. The structure, as you will see, comprises fourteen lines, the rhyme scheme being abab/cdcd/efef/gg. Each line has ten syllables, with the stress on the second syllable of each pair: Then *hate*/ me *when*/ thou *wilt*:/ if *ev*/ er, *now*. This is known as *iambic pentameter* and Shakespeare's plays are mostly written in this form: 'Once *more*/ un*to*/ the *breach*, dear *friends*,/ once *more*'; 'The /*qual*/ity/ of *mer*/cy *is*/ not *strain'd*'. You have no need to bother about the theory unless you want to. '*Poetry is the language in which man explores his own amazement,*' said Christopher Fry. You can do that just as well if you have never heard of iambic pentameter!

The following poem has always been one of my special

favourites. Study the imagery, rich and dense in keeping with the subject, and the unusual rhyme scheme.

Glory be to God for dappled things –
For skies of couple-colour as a brinded cow;
For rose-moles all in stipple upon trout that swim;
Fresh-firecoal chestnut-falls; finches' wings:
Landscape plotted and pieced – fold, fallow, and plough;
And all trades, their gear and tackle and trim.

All things counter, original, spare, strange;
Whatever is fickle, freckled (who knows how?)
With swift, slow; sweet, sour; adazzle, dim;
He fathers-forth whose beauty is past change:
Praise him.

(Pied Beauty by Gerard Manley Hopkins)

The haiku

If a sonnet seems too difficult for you to attempt at this stage, why not try the simple and delightful *haiku*? This is a poem of three lines which captures a fleeting image, a sense of beauty, wonder or sadness. It is based on a Japanese form developed in the seventeenth century and typified by the poet Basho (1643–94). The haiku (plural haiku), in the original Japanese, was a poem of seventeen syllables (5–7–5) but the English translation requires no exact wordage and your own may consist of any three short lines to suit your subject.

> 'The aimless life is the constant theme of Zen art of every kind, expressing the artist's own inner state of going nowhere in a timeless moment. All men have these moments occasionally, and it is just then that they catch those vivid glimpses of the world which cast such a glow over the intervening wastes of memory – the smell of burning leaves on a morning of autumn haze, a flight of sunlit pigeons against a thundercloud, the sound of an unseen waterfall at dusk, or the single cry of some unidentified bird in the depths of a forest . . .'
>
> (From The Way of Zen by Alan Watts)

Here are some examples:

> The thief
> left it behind –
> the moon at the window.
> > (Ryokan)

> A brushwood gate,
> and for a lock –
> this snail.
> > (Basho)

> Dozing on horseback,
> smoke from tea-fires
> drifts to the moon.
> > (Basho)

> In the dense mist,
> what is being shouted
> between hill and boat?
> > (Issa)

> A fallen flower
> returning to the branch?
> It was a butterfly
> > (Moritake)

And here are some modern haiku:

> Like an ice-cream wrapper –
> The last of summer
> Dances down the road.
> > (Ian J. Burton)

> This empty page
> Glares at me –
> White with rage.
> > (Ian J. Burton)

> The delight I feel
> goes stamping up the road in
> the little boy's coat.
> > (Colin Oliver)

'*The poet's mind,*' said T. S. Eliot, '*is in fact a receptacle for seizing and storing up numberless feelings, phrases, images, which remain there until all the particles which can unite to form a new compound are present together*' (*Tradition and the Individual Talent*).

I'd like to end with a poem by a boy of eight, one of the winners in a competition run by *The Guardian* for children's verses about Kite-flying.

> The kite like bird floats
> Gently tugging on its string
> Hands firmly keep it.
>
> Playing with the wind,
> Having a gentle tumble,
> And winks at the sun.
>
> Could we climb the string,
> And sail around in the sky,
> For always, perhaps.
>
> A dark shadow falls
> As it crosses the bright sun,
> Strange figure passes.
>
> It swoops low and high
> With its tail dancing behind,
> Then suddenly falls.
>
> Kite quiet in the grass,
> Is it dead or just sleeping?
> Let us run and see.
> (*Fly Kite* by Sam Butterfield)

His feelings, phrases and images were there all right. How about yours?

Presentation of poetry

Send out three or four poems at a time, typed centrally on sheets of A4 paper using single spacing, with double spacing between stanzas. A title sheet is not required; just put your name and address at the top right-hand side of the first sheet, with the title and the poem underneath. There is no need to state the number of words.

Exercise 13

Write *either* a sonnet *or* three haiku.

14

The Non-Fiction Book

Know your subject

Books of non-fiction are usually books of information and so you will need to be knowledgable on some subject that interests you deeply, and to supplement your existing knowledge by research. A book is rarely a success unless the author is spurred by real enthusiasm for the subject, and this special interest is bound to lead to a certain amount of reading and study before the idea of writing a book comes to mind. For instance, you wouldn't dream of attempting a cookery book unless you had been a dedicated cook for many years, or consider writing the biography of a famous tennis star if you were not a devotee of the game. It is, in my view, a mistake to 'mug-up' a subject from scratch in order to write about it. You might succeed in this way with a short article but the writing of a full-length book requires a solid background of knowledge and a deep commitment.

Textbooks

A textbook, according to the dictionary, is 'a standard book from which a particular branch of knowledge can be studied'. Books on child care, bee-keeping, sailing, yoga, calligraphy, may all be classed as textbooks.

If there are several books in print which deal with your subject – and you should read as many as you can – it is essential that you have something new and original to offer.

If no book exists on your chosen theme, then your lucky stars are shining and you must be sure to plan the book so carefully and write it so well that no publisher could refuse it.

Having decided on the book you intend to write, the first thing to do is to work out a list of chapter headings and arrange them in the best possible order. This requires a great deal of consideration. I had some difficulty, when I was planning this book, in deciding, for instance, whether to place Characterisation before or after The Short Story. I decided eventually, as you have seen, to put The Short Story first. It seemed appropriate to discuss construction (the bones) before characterisation (the flesh). However, you may think that I was wrong, bearing in mind that character is usually the most important aspect of a story.

It was obvious that How to Write an Article must come before The Radio Talk, because the guidelines for an article apply also to a talk. Some of your chapters will fall into place quite easily; others will require some juggling around before you can decide on the final sequence. Your readers are presumably coming to your book as amateurs, looking for instruction, and you must be guided by their needs. Put yourself in the student's place, picturing his difficulties and arranging your information in the most helpful way. Never forget that trial and error are part of the task; the book will have to remain in a fluid state until the last draft – which may be the fifth or sixth. At this moment, as I write Chapter 14, I have yet to decide on a final arrangement of the chapters to come. Some of the ones I had planned may have to be omitted or new ones added as the book consolidates. Each chapter can be treated in much the same way as an article, except that in some cases a rather more literary style may be employed.

It is a good idea, in the first instance, to send a list of contents, an introduction and the first three chapters (or the first two and a middle one) to a publisher in the hope of receiving a commission to write the book. (This does not apply to novels: see page 94.) Be sure that your chapters are written to the very best of your ability and choose your publisher carefully. Study the bookshops and libraries to see which publishing houses specialise in your particular type of book. You will find the addresses in the current *Writers' and Artists' Yearbook*. Enclose a covering letter giving the proposed length (it should normally be somewhere between 35 000 and 60 000 words) and explaining in some detail how you propose to tackle the subject. The publisher may well be attracted by an interesting new approach. You should also state your ideas concerning illustrations. The advice for illustrated articles in Chapter 2 applies also to non-fiction books (see page 13). Figure numbers should relate to each chapter separately (see my Figs. 18.1, 18.2 and 18.3) rather than run continuously through the book.

If the first publisher is not interested, try another. And another. Even if you are unsuccessful you may possibly receive a helpful letter, pointing out your faults and offering advice.

Technical writing (Workshop Manuals, etc.) can hardly be included in a book on creative writing, but clarity is the key word and a methodical approach is obviously required. Step-by-step instructions on, say, dismantling a carburettor must be planned with an astute awareness of the difficulties of a newcomer to the task.

Travel books

Travel books can be any length from 25 000 to 70 000 words depending to some extent on the number of illustrations. Browse in the library and study the books you admire. Needless to say, you must know and love the place you propose to write about. Planning your chapters is, once again, the best way to start, and here you will be guided by your general approach to the subject. If you have chosen Portugal, for instance, are you going to include every possible aspect of the country – history, flora and fauna, climate, agriculture, commerce, architecture, people – or are you going to take a prospective tourist on a light-hearted journey, suggesting the most beautiful and interesting places to visit? You can hardly do both. Many beginners make the mistake of including too many details; when you know your subject very well, it is a great temptation to overload your book, making it indigestible.

You will almost certainly find it necessary to spend some time on research, not only in the place concerned but also in reference libraries and museums. Your job is to unearth unusual and interesting facts, to discard those which do not fit into the scheme of your book, and to use the others with flair and charm.

Biography

The first requisite is that the man or woman you have chosen for your study has (or had) the qualifications to warrant a biography. He must inspire sufficient general interest to make the book a saleable commodity, otherwise you will be unlikely to find a publisher, however well you write it.

If your subject is still alive you will have to find out whether he is willing for you to undertake the task. You will obviously need his cooperation and you should not consider such a book until you have had a good deal of writing experience and can produce examples of your published work. It is a good idea, as with a textbook, to prepare a list of headings and three specimen chapters with a view to obtaining a commission (see page 77). Your subject will, in any case, be happier to spare you the time if a publisher is interested in the project. You will also need the help of his family and friends. It is a delicate assignment to write about the private lives of people who are still around; relatives sometimes cause serious problems for the writer by wanting him to distort the truth. This you must never do, but I think you should respect their wishes – there may be factors unknown to you which colour their attitudes – and you may decide to abandon the project rather than drain the life-blood out of your work.

Let us assume that all goes well. Consider the biographies you have read and decide on your own approach. Is it to be a long, scholarly book or a shorter, more buoyant one? The aim of a biography is to present a truthful and readable account of the person concerned, so you will begin by talking to him and making notes on every aspect of his life which is relevant to the book you have in mind. Many interviews will be necessary; be sure not to tire him by staying too long at a time (see Chapter 15). You will probably need to spend, in all, a great many hours with him; sometimes a biographer who lives some distance away will arrange to stay for a while in the subject's house or in a nearby hotel. You will also arrange to meet as many of his relatives, friends and associates as possible. Small incidents, mentioned in conversation, may shed new light on his character and add depth to your book.

You might be interested in the possibility of 'ghost writing'. A well-known personality who does not possess the necessary skills to write a book may wish to publish his 'autobiography', done in such a way that the reader will assume he has written it himself. The ghost writer goes about his task in much the same way as the biographer except that the book is written in the first person from the subject's point of view and the name of the real author does not appear. Royalties are shared by mutual agreement. You may question the ethics of all this, as I do, but there are a great many books of this kind on sale.

If you want to write about a man or a woman who is dead, find out from the reference library if other biographies have appeared. If so, read them all diligently. If you think you can produce a new one with sufficient fresh appeal to interest a publisher, begin your research, making notes and assembling your information in chronological order. Sort out your points, as you would do for an article, deciding where to start and how to lead on smoothly and logically to the end.

Autobiography

Successful autobiographies are usually written by people who have done something of outstanding significance – sailed the Atlantic single-handed, made their name on the stage or in Parliament, survived a heart transplant, run a leper colony. Failing such distinction, they can write with such humour (e.g. Margaret Powell) or with such literary style (e.g. Laurie Lee) that the simplest incidents become absorbing. It is very rare indeed for the average person, even though he writes extremely well, to get his autobiography accepted for publication.

Many of my students have told me about their exciting lives – teaching in Africa, serving as air raid wardens in the London Blitz, going on cruises round the world – hoping that I shall encourage them to write their autobigraphies. I hate to have to tell them that hundreds of people have done these things and that it requires a very special talent to write a publishable book on experiences which, although they are of great significance to the person concerned, are not sufficiently outstanding. Perhaps you have that special talent; if so let nothing deter you. In any case, your rich experiences will provide material for articles. Another possibility is to use them as background in a novel. Many famous writers have utilised their travels in this way – notably Somerset Maugham, H. E. Bates, Graham Greene, Paul Scott. In this case you will create a fictitious story and imaginary characters; on no account be tempted to put *yourself* into the novel, merely disguising your identity by changing your name! It is a grave mistake, in almost every case, to put real people into fiction (see page 47).

You may feel that you would like to write the story of your life for the benefit of your children and grandchildren. This, of course, is a delightful enterprise, so long as you have no expectations of getting it published. However, it will be much more satisfying to you – and to your readers – if the book is well-planned and well-written. Beware of including too many trivial incidents and personal opinions. Select the most significant aspects of your life and write them up in a lively style, dividing the book into chapters of not more than 2500 words. Sometimes a novice will continue without a break – sometimes without a new paragraph – for thirty pages or so. No grandchild would ever stay the course!

Collaboration

My very first book was written in collaboration with a friend. We discovered, by chance, that there was no book on stamp-collecting for very young children. They often handle stamps with jammy fingers, stick them into albums with glue, and fail to appreciate their beauty and delicacy. Kay Horowicz and I wanted to remedy this and we decided to write a book for five to seven year-olds entitled *Fun with Stamps*. She was an expert philatelist with a valuable collection, but not a writer; I only collected stamps in a half-hearted fashion but I had become successful in selling articles. Neither of us could have written the book alone but together we thought we could do it. It was published by Hutchinson in 1957 and stayed in print for twenty years!

We worked on a fifty-fifty basis all along, sharing the work, the expenses and – later – the royalties. She supplied the information in note form, and I wrote it up. I had never written for that age-group but I studied the market and it worked. Kay died many years ago but she will always live in those pages and I shall never forget the happy hours we spent with our heads together, comparing notes until we were both quite satisfied that we had done the best we could.

Perhaps, as I did, you can find someone with specialised knowledge who is willing to join forces so that you can produce a book together. If you live near to your collaborator, so much the better, but you can work by post if need be.

Presentation of manuscripts

Books should be typed in the same way as short stories (double spacing on good quality A4 paper, with generous margins, etc.) but serial rights do not apply and your title sheet must bear no reference to them. When you sell a book, the terms are stated in a publisher's contract which you will sign when the negotiations are completed (see page 123).

If you need to add material after your book is typed you may number additional pages 37A, 37B and so on – but don't do it too often! There is no need to bind your typescript, though you may clip the pages of each chapter together with slide-on clips. Most publishers prefer loose pages so they can easily be separated (the editor might wish to put part of your book in his briefcase to read in the train). The best thing to do is to put the manuscript in a typing-paper box, making sure that the pages are in the correct order. It's easy and it's professional. A publisher once told me about a typescript he had received which was bound in leather with the title and the author's name beautifully tooled on the cover. (It was a terrible book, as he had expected it to be!) Every publisher's dream is to discover a brilliant new author, and your MS will certainly be studied with care and interest. This does not mean that all type-scripts are read from beginning to end. A professional reader can discern from the first few pages whether or not a book is likely to be publishable.

You should always send a preliminary letter before you submit a manuscript to a publisher; it may be that he no longer requires the kind of book you have to offer, his lists may be full or he might recently have accepted a similar work. It is in your own interest, as well as his, to make sure that your MS will be welcome. Write a *very brief* letter stating the category, title and length of your book and asking if he would be willing to consider it. If you receive the go-ahead, send your typescript with a (very brief) covering letter thanking him for his interest and saying that you now enclose your book entitled so-and-so and you hope that he will like it. You should attach a gummed self-addressed label bearing the correct postage for its return if unsuitable. You might also enclose a stamped addressed postcard and re-quest acknowledgment; some publishers, regrettably, have become rather lax about such courtesies. Send your parcel by Registered Post or Recorded Delivery and be prepared to wait at least two months for a decision. During that time do not write or telephone and *on no account* pay a personal visit. Try to forget about the book and get on with the next one, although your heart will probably jump every time you hear the postman!

Exercise 14

Work out a list of chapter headings for the non-fiction book you feel most qualified to write.

15

How to Conduct an Interview

In order to write a full-length biography of a living person, or even a short biographical article for a staff or college magazine, you will need to know something about the art of interviewing. If you have ever been interviewed yourself, you will already know how to do it – or how *not* to do it!

Your first move is to write to (or telephone) the person concerned, asking if he or she would be willing to be interviewed and giving three or four possible dates. If you receive a favourable reply, write back at once, thanking him for his kindness and mentioning the agreed date once again in case he has mislaid the correspondence. Having got so far, telephone a day or two before the appointment to ask if he is agreeable to your using a tape recorder. Some people hate to think that their every word is captured for replay, so don't be surprised if the answer is no. If your request is refused, don't betray the slightest disappointment. Merely say, that's quite all right, you understand. It is very important to establish an easy relationship right from the start.

If the interviewee does agree to be taped, you should still be prepared to use only a notebook and pencil. Not only is there a possibility of the machine breaking down, but there is also the chance that your subject may take fright at the last moment. Arm yourself with a good supply of paper and pencils, and if, like me, you know nothing of shorthand, put in some practice at writing very quickly in your own abbreviated longhand. Arrange a mock interview with a friend, jotting down his answers with all possible speed and making sure that you can decipher your scribble afterwards.

Do your 'homework' thoroughly. Read everything you can about the person concerned and plan your questions carefully. Twelve is a good number. Consider what you yourself would like to know and you can be fairly sure that your readers will have similar interests. Arrange your questions in a logical order, paying special attention to the first one, which should be designed to put the interviewee at his ease.

Don't arrive late – nor yet too early. Even someone famous and self-assured may well be apprehensive on this occasion. Assume a relaxed and confident manner yourself even though you may feel that you are far more nervous than he is. *Never* apologise for your inexperience or belittle yourself in any way.

Whatever answers you receive to your questions, do not be drawn into an argument. You are there to talk about *him* and *his* views, not your own, and you should in fact say very little. If you feel he is being evasive on some important point, be courteous but firm in pressing for a satisfactory reply, but if you sense that your persistence is causing embarrassment, move on to another question. (Some writers send their questions in advance but this is a matter for you and your particular subject. The spontaneous approach will usually elicit livelier replies.)

Don't stay too long. However well things are going, an hour and a half is about as much as anyone should be expected to take. I must admit that I enjoy being interviewed but some people dislike it. You will soon see which are which and conduct your interview accordingly.

If you use a tape recorder, test it out just before you start; other people's electric sockets or wiring can be faulty and it might be safer to use new batteries. If you take notes, whether in shorthand or longhand, you would be wise to write them out in detail *the very moment you get home*. You will then recall additional points you couldn't get down on paper. Writing up a biographical piece from pages of notes is a demanding task at the best of times, but your work will be very much easier if you expand your jottings while the encounter is fresh in your memory.

Your subject will very much appreciate the opportunity to

check the typescript for errors before you offer it for publication. You might have made a factual mistake or mis-spelt a proper name. Tell him you will send him a copy, and explain that it must be returned to you at once or there will not be time for you to amend it. Newspaper journalists have too tight a schedule to allow for corrections but if you wish to write a magazine article or a full length biography you can usually allow time for checking to ensure that your account is completely accurate.

Exercise 15

Choose a friend who is willing to be the subject of a practice interview and prepare twelve suitable questions.

16

The Novel

The challenge

Writing a novel is one of the greatest challenges in the whole field of creative writing. It is exciting, demanding, exhausting – and deeply satisfying. There may be times when you feel you can't go on, but an inner voice will urge you to continue and if you pay attention to that voice you will somehow find the way forward. Every writer experiences frustration and hopelessness at times; the measure of your quality as a novelist is not only your imagination and your skill with words, but also your ability to persevere in the face of discouragement, to work until the pages gradually build up into a weighty pile and your book is finished.

For the purpose of this chapter we will discuss the so-called 'straight' novel, one which does not fall easily into any other category. There are, of course, many different kinds of novels – romances, science fiction, crime, teenage and so on – but I hope these guidelines will help you with whatever type you wish to write. If you decide to start an historical romance, for instance, I would advise you to read a selection of the best available and study the length, construction and style. A straight novel may be anything from 60 000 to 100 000 words and thirty chapters of roughly 2500 would give you a good average length of 75 000. Other categories vary, and you must be sure to write to an appropriate length if you want to see your work in print. (Some novelists prefer to divide their books into unnumbered sections rather than chapters but it might be wise to choose the traditional approach for your first novel.)

Publishers, for the most part, specialise in certain types of books and have 'slots' to fill. One of the most common reasons for refusal is that a novel 'falls between two stools'. It might be basically a romantic novel, for instance, but if it includes erotic scenes which might offend the average reader of romantic fiction it would be virtually unpublishable; likewise a detective story with a love interest so strong that the book is neither a who-dun-it nor a romance. Most of us deplore these restrictions but they are an established part of the publishing world and you would be wise to heed them unless you are a writer of such brilliance that you can create your own category and take the world by storm, as Richard Adams did with *Watership Down* – after many rejections!

Before you begin a novel you might ask yourself the questions in the following sections. Finding the answers will help you to plan your book.

The theme

What is the story to be about?
In other words, what is the theme? The plot can develop later, but the theme is a matter for consideration at the outset. It can often be summed up in a single word or a short phrase: for example, betrayal, revenge, the need for independence. A book without a theme can become a mere sequence of events with no foundation, no real reason for its existence. The theme you choose should be one that concerns you deeply. It will almost certainly be close to your own experience but beware of writing an autobiography. You should change the characters and the situations, using your imagination to create a fictitious drama. If you put yourself into a novel you will be tempted to include too many real events, losing the essential qualities of art and invention. Fiction has the appearance of reality but it must have relevance and suspense, combined into a shapely whole.

The more deeply you are affected by your theme, even to the point of obsession, the more likely you are to produce a successful book. Many of us write novels to explore the problems that trouble us, so don't be afraid to tackle a disturbing theme. Your story may be sparked off by an image – a picture of two people in confrontation, a situation of great delicacy or danger, or simply an arresting face. From this starting point you are swept into a story which builds up more and more strongly in your imagination. In cases like this, your theme may only become apparent as you progress, but you will need to keep it constantly in mind. If you lose sight of the theme you may lose that sense of unity and power which is so vital to the structure of the book.

The central character

Whose story is it?
The choice of a central character is perhaps the most important aspect of your book. This is the person your reader must care about – and care very deeply – if he is to feel involved in the story. When we read fiction we like to identify with the main character, even though he or she may be quite different from ourselves.

As with the short story, many amateur novels are spoiled because the author chose the wrong central character. Let's say your theme is the need for independence. A woman is filled with resentment against her selfish and domineering father because he tries to prevent her from marrying the man she loves. This must surely be the woman's story. The reader will be led to identify with her, suffer with her, care about her happiness. The father's attitude will no doubt be explained and we shall understand what drives him to behave as he does, but it would be a grave mistake, in my opinion, for the author to choose him as the central character because he would not claim the reader's sympathy.

Having decided whose story it is, you should pause to consider the next important question.

What is this person's problem?
'Why does everyone have to have a *problem*?' you may ask. The answer is that there must be conflict or there can be no drama, no suspense, no readability. When you read the opening pages of a good novel, of whatever kind, you are

drawn into the story, engrossed, eager to know the outcome. This is almost certainly because the author has presented *a person with a problem*.

The problem faced by your hero or heroine provides the story line for the novel. It is closely bound up with the question *What is the story to be about*? As the book progresses, you will drive your hero to the limits of his endurance and show the gradual development of his character. The more deeply you ponder on the problems of your characters the more you will understand about human nature. Sometimes you may find that you 'write better than you know' and look back on certain scenes with surprise and delight, marvelling at your own perception. This is a happy by-product of novel-writing: in analysing the problems of our characters we may quite unexpectedly come upon solutions to our own.

Setting

Where does it happen?
Choose localities which are close to your own experience. You will need to introduce a variety of backgrounds – the reader soon tires of the same venue – and your theme will indicate those that are appropriate to the story. Unusual settings are naturally intriguing and you should dream up a happy blend of the familiar and the exceptional (see Chapter 11).

When does it happen?
Before you begin your novel you will need to consider the range of your book. Is the action to take place in one dramatic weekend or to cover two generations? A family saga, for instance, must be very carefully planned if you are to avoid a sprawling construction, even though you may find, as you write, that the time-span has to be increased or reduced. A story which occupies only a month is less of a problem, but in all cases I suggest that you bear in mind exactly *when* each scene is taking place.

It is not always easy to remember what day it is in your

novel and I find it helpful to make a pencil note at the beginning of each chapter or section (e.g. 'First Saturday', 'Second Thursday', 'Christmas Eve'). Changes in the weather will help you to establish a compact time-structure; heat-waves, wintry spells, gales and thunderstorms serve not only to bring atmosphere and drama into your story but also to chronicle the passing days. A confused reader is a disgruntled reader so do take care to let him know at all times *Who* it is, *Where* it is and *When* it is.

If you are writing an historical novel you will already be well informed about the period you have chosen, but some research is sure to be necessary; you will need to spend a good deal of time in reference libraries and museums as well as poring over library books at home. Accuracy is vital. The reader's 'willing suspension of disbelief', on which all novelists rely, will be destroyed if you allow even one anachronism to slip into your story.

Construction

Where are you going to start?

I think it is true to say that this is one of the most difficult decisions any novelist has to make: at what point in the life of your main character are you to begin your story? If something of great importance occurred in his childhood, will you start with that scene in direct narrative or describe it later in flashback? Sometimes you can only solve the problem by trial and error. Flashback can be effective but it should be used sparingly; immediate action is usually much more telling than retrospect. 'John took a deep breath and threw himself into the fast-moving torrent twenty feet below' is more dramatic than 'John told me how he had taken a deep breath and thrown himself into the fast-moving torrent twenty feet below' or 'John remembered how he had . . . etc.' Always 'make a scene of it' (a favourite maxim of mine) unless there are good reasons for doing otherwise. If you insert a section of flashback be sure to make the transition perfectly clear. Bear in mind that you yourself know exactly what is happening, and when, because you invented it, whereas the reader knows only what he is told.

Your first chapter should contain a big scene – or the build-up to a big scene in Chapter 2. It will probably be a confrontation between the main character and a person or situation. This conflict will embody the theme – the problem which is at the heart of your story. As a general rule, you should introduce your hero or heroine on page 1; in this way you will devise a compelling opening in which the reader identifies with him or her and hopes for a happy outcome. What the outcome is, he will only discover by following your story *to the very end*.

Viewpoint

I have touched on this question in Chapter 6. Your decision will have an important bearing on construction. If you choose the first person, you will find it easier to hold your novel within a tight framework, but there are obvious limitations: nothing can happen which is not known to your central character. If you employ the third person but adhere to one viewpoint throughout the book, you have this same problem, of course, but again it produces a strong construction. The most usual method is to write in the third person, choosing three or four viewpoint characters so that the events are seen from different angles. If you decide on this approach you will have to plan your scenes carefully, ringing the changes with a nice feeling for balance as well as drama. It is, in my opinion, a great mistake to introduce more than one viewpoint in each chapter or scene.

'Why,' you may ask, 'can't I have a God's-eye view of all the characters, knowing and saying what they are thinking?' This is a question I often hear and my answer is this: if you leap in and out of the various characters' minds you will fragment the power of the scene and destroy its unity. Many published writers do this very thing and I can only wish they wouldn't! You will, of course, see your whole grouping objectively, but you would be wise to remain behind the eyes of your chosen character within each scene unless you have a special reason for doing otherwise.

Plot

I dislike the word 'plot' – it suggests a contrived situation – but your book must have a strong backbone. One of the most common failings in amateur novels is a looseness of construction which allows the story line to be lost in a welter of irrelevancies (see page 34 on *Suspense*). You must preserve the shape by sticking resolutely to the tale you have decided to tell, refusing to be tempted down pathways which, although attractive, lead away from the central theme. You need to tell a good story and you will find that it develops with surprising continuity, one scene growing out of another, if you allow your characters, with their individual predicaments, to lead you onwards, page by page. Try to write your novel every day, even if only for an hour or so. If you keep in touch with the narrative you will find the task much easier.

The ending

I seldom know how my novels are going to end until I get there. In my third book, *Kick a Tin Can*, I literally didn't know until I was writing the last page but one! Some novelists (Iris Murdoch, for instance) plan the story in great detail before they begin to write. Others work as I do, letting the original concept change and develop as they go along. John Fowles does not plan. '*I begin*,' he says, '*with an image, a ghost of an idea, nothing more, not knowing where it will lead.*' Choose the way that suits you best; it's the quality of the finished book that counts.

As with the short story, beware of anti-climax. When you have brought your hero to the end of a particular phase in his life and resolved his problem, then it is time to stop.

Dramatising a situation

The following extract from my book *The Craft of Novel-Writing* may be helpful:

'First of all, make sure that the situation you have in mind is credible and that it is vital to this novel. Then, having decided at what point in the narrative the particular situation is to occur, lead up to it with care, creating the right atmosphere and mood. The situation might be completely unexpected but it will be convincing if you have prepared the way for it. The leading-up paragraphs, although less dramatic in themselves, make the moments of drama more telling and significant, not only by contrast, but because you are subtly building up the tension; the reader senses the approach of the storm in the stillness that precedes it.

Sometimes the preparation for a dramatic situation might begin a dozen chapters earlier – or even on the first page of the novel. Death is more tragic if the person who dies was deeply loved; joy is more intense after despair; betrayal more terrible after perfect trust . . . Seize every chance for added drama, so long as everything is relevant and has, for you, the ring of truth. Make a conscious effort to intrigue and excite the reader so that your own involvement is transmitted to him and he is moved as you are moved.'

In the book I have written on many aspects of the subject which cannot be included in a single chapter, and you may like to read it before you embark on a novel.

Presentation of manuscripts

Novels are presented in much the same way as non-fiction books (see page 82). For your first novel, however, you should submit the whole book rather than a synopsis and the first two or three chapters. No publisher can rely on a new novelist to sustain the promise of a good opening; he has to be sure before he can offer a contract.

Exercise 16

If you have in mind a novel you would like to write, answer the preceding six questions in note form.

17

Writing for Children

The readership

People sometimes think that writing for children is 'an easy way to start' but nothing could be further from the truth: it is a very specialised form of writing and demands great insight and skill. Perhaps it is considered to be easy for the following reasons: the writer does not require a large vocabulary; books for young people are usually shorter than those for adults; a child will listen with rapt attention to almost any story, giving the amateur writer a sense of euphoria which is not always justified. ('My little granddaughter loved it and wanted more' does not necessarily mean that a publisher will feel the same!)

In general you need to have some idea of the age of your readers and yet, on a higher level, the best children's writers simply *write*, addressing themselves to another human being, of whatever age, who will respond with pleasure. '*Whatever you have in hand, write it as simply as you can, and the material itself will dictate the nature of the audience,*' says the well-loved author Jill Paton Walsh. The famous classics which shine as examples to us all, are read and enjoyed by anyone from eight to eighty and in some ways that makes a nonsense of dividing your readers into groups. After all, a bright seven-year-old can enjoy stories written for teen-agers, and a young adult of sixteen who is not a natural reader may prefer a book which was written with a much younger person in mind.

I think you must feel at ease with children – indeed, have

a childlike quality in your own nature – in order to write for them successfully. You should also be closely in touch with the youngsters of today, however clearly you recall your own childhood. Things are very different now.

Your first task, whatever age-group you have in mind, is to visit the children's departments of bookshops and libraries, studying the length, format and subject matter of the books which are popular, those which are most frequently bought and borrowed. Talk to teachers and librarians, but most of all – *talk to children*. Ask them what they enjoy the most, and why. Read their favourite authors and find out what it is that makes the books appealing. One thing is certain: you will discover that successful writers never 'talk down'; the slightest hint of a patronising or moralising approach will ruin your chances of success.

Fiction

It is very important to keep the action going and make sure that there is excitement on every page. This applies to the domestic story which is closely related to the reader's experience as well as to thrillers, science-fiction, fantasy and adventure. Movement and colour are key words for children's fiction and you must present your story in a way which will grip the attention on the very first page and hold it till the last. Short sentences, short paragraphs and short chapters will help to achieve this result. The time and place must be unmistakable and the characters clearly defined. Beginners often make the mistake of writing about a child who lacks individuality – kind, intelligent, good-looking, but in no way *unique*. Think about your young characters as deeply as you would for an adult story and create a hero or heroine who comes to life as a full-blooded person with strong individuality. Readers like to identify with the main character so choose a child who is a little older than your intended readership.

Animals are perennial favourites. Any creature from a tortoise to a pterodactyl will be taken to a child's heart if you tell a good story about it and appreciate the need for distinct animal characterisation.

'The first rabbit stopped in a sunny patch and scratched his ear with rapid movements of his hind-leg . . . He looked as though he knew how to take care of himself. There was a shrewd, buoyant air about him as he sat up, looked around and rubbed both front paws over his nose. As soon as he was satisfied that all was well, he laid back his ears and set to work on the grass.

His companion seemed less at ease. He was small, with wide, staring eyes and a way of raising and turning his head which suggested not so much caution as a kind of ceaseless, nervous tension. His nose moved continually and when a bumble-bee flew humming to a thistle bloom behind him, he jumped and spun round with a start that sent two nearby rabbits scurrying for holes before the nearest, a buck with black-tipped ears, recognised him and returned to feeding.

"Oh, it's only Fiver," said the black-tipped rabbit, "jumping at blue-bottles again . . ."'

(From *Watership Down* by Richard Adams)

' "Don't do that. Please don't do that!"
Sprog raised the stone above his head.

"I don't mean you any harm. Please don't throw that stone."

He stared unbelievingly at the creature. "Are you a dragon?" he asked fearfully.

"What's a dragon?" The mournful eyes gazed at him.

"Well, it's a – " Sprog searched for the right words. "I don't know really, but you do look very much like one. At least – er, how much more of you is there underneath the water?"

The creature glanced down. "Quite a lot."

"Can you breathe fire?"

"I'm not sure. I've never tried. Quite honestly, I don't really feel like trying, not just now. I haven't been at all well lately."

"I'm sorry to hear that," said Sprog politely. "I hope it's nothing serious?"

"The most frightful toothache. I've hardly been able to get any sleep at all. Can you see anything?" It opened

its mouth wide, revealing a hideous array of teeth.
Sprog pressed back against the cave wall again. "It's
somewhere around the left-hand side at the bottom,
towards the back."'

(From *A Dinosaur Called Minerva* by Tessa Krailing)

Always introduce plenty of dialogue, but beware of slang
that will date. Avoid four-letter words; children don't mind
them in the least but parents and teachers do. Introduce
your characters one at a time, don't have too many, and bear
in mind that youngsters like their 'goodies' and 'baddies'
quite distinct so that they know for certain whose side to be
on. Right must always triumph in the end and the young
hero (or heroine) should find a way out of his difficulties *by
his own efforts*; never let an adult be the one to sort things
out. The days are past, thank goodness, when parents,
teachers and policemen had to be portrayed as beyond
reproach. Children read the papers and watch television and
when they read stories about the real world, they want truth
not hypocrisy. They are upset by too much suffering and
distress for the main character if he is a child like themselves
but they enjoy horror if it is not too close to their own
experience. A child will be far more distraught while reading
about a little boy who loses his mother on a railway station
than about a pirate who is boiled in oil!

Humour is important but remember that young children
do not understand sarcasm. They all love slap-stick and revel
(like the rest of us) in the downfall of unpleasant people in
authority.

On the whole, children prefer happy endings; whenever I
give a talk at a school I ask for a show of hands on this
question. I also ask about first or third person narrative and
it seems they have no preference provided it's a good story
and they can easily relate to the main character.

Description must be kept to a minimum and introduced in
small doses, interspersed with plenty of action and dialogue.
In order to make your images vivid and colourful you may
find it helpful to picture your scenes in terms of illustrations
for the book; you need a strong visual approach when you
are writing for young people. Above all, write with clarity

and simplicity. And that, of course, is good advice for creative writing in general.

There is not a big demand for children's short stories, but the length may be anything from 500 to 2000 words. You might find success with a book of stories about the same people, all self-contained but revolving around the adventures of two or three central characters. Strip cartoon stories for the so-called 'comics' are always in demand, but this is a very specialised field and you should study the various periodicals. The text must obviously be married to the illustrations, which will be separately commissioned, and you will probably need some editorial advice before you attempt such a project.

Novels for children (as opposed to those for young adults, which are considered at the end of this chapter) range from 10 000 to 30 000 words depending on the type of book and the age-group. Take a notebook along to the library and make a thorough investigation before you plan your book in detail.

Non-fiction

Here again there is an endless variety of subjects to choose from: sports, hobbies, pets, exploration, making things, and learning exciting new facts about almost anything – from the way a spider weaves its web to the rings of Saturn. Whatever you decide upon, it must be written in a direct, lively style, friendly and conversational, with all your facts logically and clearly presented. If you can write on a subject which has not yet been covered for children, you are in a splendid position to produce a successful book.

Apart from books, there is a place for short articles of 1000 words or so in annuals, in some of the 'comics' and on the children's pages of various periodicals. Consult the *Writers' and Artists' Yearbook* for current requirements. There is also a demand for talks in schools broadcasting (see Chapter 3). Always state your qualifications for writing on specialised subjects.

The under-sevens

Hardback books are ideal for small children, not only because they are durable but because the child will learn from an early age to handle books with care and keep them (relatively) free from chocolate and peanut-butter. Books of this kind are mainly story books (although there is a need for entertaining non-fiction) and they are always copiously illustrated. This means that the text must be written accordingly and is usually quite short – sometimes only half a dozen words to a page. The length of a picture-book story may be anything from 500 to 2000 words, and the royalties are shared between author and artist.

As a writer you need only concern yourself with the words, but consider the plan of the page spreads; your wording must give rise to suitable illustrations at regular intervals. The publisher will organise the pictures if he accepts your manuscript, although your suggestions will receive careful consideration. If you are an outstanding artist as well as a writer, you could produce a complete book, but the art work must obviously be of a highly professional standard. If you qualify, keep the text quite separate from the illustrations, indicating the position of the pictures by marginal notes. (It is advisable, if you are undecided about your artistic prowess, to submit the text with two or three specimen drawings or paintings, asking whether they are suitable.)

In writing for the under-sevens, the words you use should, in general, fall within the normal vocabulary of a five-year-old, but the occasional long word will give the story an added zest provided that the word is not vital to the meaning. For example, '*Susan saw an adolescent boy climb into the boat*' would be wrong, but '*Susan saw the boat rock perilously as the little boy jumped into it*' is quite acceptable. A child who doesn't understand the word 'adolescent' cannot picture the scene correctly, whereas the meaning of 'perilously' is implicit in the phrase and can be skipped, although the reader (or listener) will probably remember the word and expand his vocabulary.

Books containing separate stories about the same characters, either human or animal, are especially popular with the very young and lend themselves to bedtime reading. A dozen stories of 800 words each – about five minutes reading time – would be a suitable length.

The market for short pieces for the under-sevens is limited to annuals, 'comics', the children's pages of a few periodicals, and some radio programmes. Study the markets carefully and tailor your work accordingly. The length required is usually under 1000 words.

Young adults

I avoid the word 'teenager' as far as possible because the people concerned dislike it themselves. This is another question I have raised with school audiences and 'Young Adults' seems to be the description they prefer. 'Under Twenties' also finds some favour.

Short stories for this age-group are confined almost exclusively to magazines for girls. There is usually a strong love interest and some periodicals use only 'confession' stories. These are written in the first person without a by-line and illustrated with photographs, giving the impression that the writer herself is actually the girl in the story. The length varies from 1000 to 5000 words, depending on the magazine. It is advisable to read a good selection before attempting to write one.

Novels for young adults are also read mainly by girls. Boys of this age usually prefer adult books by such authors as Alistair MacLean and Frederick Forsyth. Nevertheless, there is some demand for boys' novels with a background of sport, mystery, adventure, science fiction and so on, and they require a strong story line with plenty of action and suspense. The length of a so-called 'teenage novel' is between 25000 and 40000 words, and the main difference from an adult novel, apart from the length, is that the main character should be about sixteen and there must be movement and dialogue all the way, with a minimum of description and introspection. Books for this market often earn high rewards as they are bought by school libraries and may be circulated in book clubs. Writing for this age-group is rewarding in other ways as well; a good novel can develop the habit of reading in a child whose home contains no books, and the characters and events you describe will stick in the memory. If you write an absorbing tale with warmth and understanding you will give your readers something of value to think about, long after the excitement of the story is forgotten.

Don't write for young adults unless you sympathise with their problems and understand their attitudes. If you have no under-twenties in your family try to form friendships with as many as possible, talking seriously about the matters which concern them. Read teenage novels, watch television programmes for and about them, and listen to pop stations on the radio, paying special attention to the patter of the disc jockeys. They have the right approach – treating their young listeners as equals and not being afraid to admit their own weaknesses. People under twenty are usually insecure and welcome the knowledge that adults, too, can be nervous and anxious. Bring this out in your stories and the readers will warm to you.

Almost any subject is permissible, with the eternal proviso that it is treated with delicacy and compassion. There is no need to avoid scenes of strong emotion. Fear, love, jealousy and hatred play their part in most young lives, and to leave them out would be just as grave a mistake as to give them too much emphasis. Youngsters who are going through a disturbed period in their lives, often with no one to confide in, can be comforted and helped by stories which deal sympathetically with problems similar to their own.

Exercise 17

Either write a story of 800 words for a child under seven, creating a character, either animal or human, which will inspire deep affection in the reader, *or* write Exercise 16 having in mind a novel for young adults.

18

Plays

Advice on the presentation of manuscripts appears at the end of the chapter.

The stage play

Thornton Wilder, the well-known American author of both plays and novels, had this to say: *'I regard the theatre as the greatest of all art forms, the most immediate way in which a human being can share with another the sense of what it is to be a human being. This supremacy of the theatre derives from the fact that it is always "Now" on the stage.'*

We all know the delightful sense of anticipation we feel when we are waiting for a play to begin, the excitement when the lights go down and the curtain rises (if there *is* a curtain) on the first scene. The theatre-goer is eager to be entertained, having taken the trouble to make the journey, and your task as a playwright is to put yourself in his place and make sure that he feels a sense of involvement from the very beginning. You must be constantly aware of the need to keep him intrigued, whether your play is a thriller, a comedy or a drama. One of the secrets is to watch out for any passages of inessential dialogue and ruthlessly prune them away. If a word can be dispensed with and still leave the play intact, then it must go.

Be careful not to introduce into the first five minutes any information so vital that the play would lose its meaning for a late-comer. You may think, as I do, that anyone who arrives after a play has begun should not be admitted until the first interval, but this is a point to bear in mind when you write the opening pages. Beware, too, of feeding information to the audience in an obvious way, making your characters tell each other things they know perfectly well already ('After all, I'm your son.'; 'We've only been here since Friday.') One way of overcoming this problem is to introduce a newcomer who, like the audience, has to know who's who and what's going on.

Most plays deal with *one main problem* and you should start, as in the short story and the novel, at a moment which heralds the first impact of that problem. Plays, perhaps more than any other form of fiction, need convincing and exciting characterisation. The actors will obviously interpret and bring to life the characters you create but they cannot do it *unless you give them the words*. Consider every aspect of the dialogue, not only what the people say but how much they say, how they say it and to whom they talk most easily and honestly. We all know how certain people encourage communication and others block it. The blocking of communication is one of the greatest causes of conflict in a play (as in real life!) and you must use your skills to build up tension in your audience through the clash of personalities as well as through the action itself. In general, keep your speeches fairly short (there will, of course, be exceptions) and remember that people have a habit of interrupting one another, especially when they are angry or distressed. Avoid party chatter and charlady chatter; it may be amusing but if it doesn't contribute to the development of the story it has no place in your play (see Chapter 10).

The audience must be made to care at all times about what happens to the people on stage. As in a novel, there must be surprises combined with a sense of truth and inevitability. Emotions will run high from time to time; allow your characters to express their feelings strongly, not only in words but in actions. (You'll never be a successful playwright if you are hampered by inhibitions!) Establish your characters in good time so that members of the audience don't have to whisper to one another 'Who's that – his wife or his sister?' The time and place must always be clear; there should really be no need for a programme to proclaim that it is Helen's bedroom the next morning or Simon's study three weeks later.

There is a great deal of sheer *craft* involved in writing for the theatre; you must be aware of the producer, the actors, the stage and the audience as well as the structure of your play and the reality of your story. Join a dramatic society if you can; this will help you to keep in touch with the mechanics of the theatre and avoid the mistakes so often made by new writers. You will learn how to organise changes of scene if you need them, how to get your characters on and off stage, how to write dialogue which is *speakable*. You will make sure that even the smallest part is interesting to play and you will allow time for the actors to change their costumes if necessary between appearances. These things may seem obvious but you'd be surprised how many beginners forget them. Keep your stage directions to the bare essentials. That's the producer's job and the author should bow to his wishes as far as possible.

Remember that your play is much more likely to be accepted if it is not expensive to produce, so avoid period costume, large casts and elaborate sets. You have no need to feel inhibited on account of economic restrictions; this can be a discipline which enhances your writing. The real quality of a play depends upon *character* and *suspense*. Read as many plays as you can, both old and new; there is normally a good selection in the public libraries. You would also find it helpful to read *Amateur Theatre* by Jennifer Curry, published in this series. The amateur stage is the most promising opening for the new playwright.

The one-act play – most suitable of all for a first attempt – may be compared with the short story and lasts from thirty to forty-five minutes. You should limit your cast to a maximum of six and concentrate on one dominant dramatic situation. The three-act play, which is more like a novel in concept, may include one or two sub-plots (provided they are related to the main theme) and there is time for a more gradual development. It lasts about two and a half hours and may not in fact be divided into three acts so long as there is at least one interval. The length of the intervals will be decided by the theatre management. In the traditional three-act play each act lasts for roughly forty-five minutes and comprises no more than three scenes. The first act is usually the longest, the last the shortest. You might have up to ten characters but a smaller cast is easier to handle when you are inexperienced, quite apart from the cost of production.

The final line of a play is often written in such a way as to clarify the theme, so that the playgoer leaves the theatre with a certain phrase ringing in his head, a phrase that will stick in the memory. You may even find it helpful to write the last line first!

The following plays would form a good basis for study: *Dear Octopus* by Dodie Smith; *Dangerous Corner* by J. B. Priestley; *The Deep Blue Sea* by Terence Rattigan; *Look Back in Anger* by John Osborne; *The Caretaker* by Harold Pinter; *Abigail's Party* by Mike Leigh.

There is a valuable section on *Markets for Plays* in the *Writers' and Artists' Yearbook*. You might also look at periodicals connected with the stage to learn about current requirements, competitions and so on. For a specimen layout see Fig. 18.1.

The radio play

The possibilities are endless. At no extra cost you can set your scene in medieval Britain, on a tropical island, in an aircraft flying over the South Pole or at the top of the Eiffel Tower. All the listener has to do is to close his eyes and allow you to take him there. All *you* have to do is to fill those blank sheets of A4 paper with the right sounds and speeches. And here I can offer you real encouragement: radio plays from new authors will always be required. The craft is specialised but not too difficult to master if you have a good story to tell and a gift for writing dialogue. When I was a comparative beginner I took a correspondence course on radio drama and before I finished the course I had sold a half-hour play to the BBC. You might do the same.

Now let's get down to the practicalities. A radio play *must* be written specially for the medium. It's no use sending a stage play to the BBC in the hope that they will fall in love with it and adapt it themselves. You must learn the techniques and produce a typescript which proves that you know your job.

Radio plays are divided into sequences in much the same way as television plays are divided into scenes. Radio is for

MAURICE (<u>angrily</u>): You'd better get on the phone and cancel that booking this minute.

ANN: But I need a holiday - I'll have a nervous breakdown if I don't get away -

MAURICE: If you cancel now there won't be anything to pay -

ANN: Pay! Pay! All you think about is money - .

MAURICE: Pick up that phone!

ANN: You don't <u>listen</u> to me - you've <u>never</u> listened to me -

MAURICE: Are you going to phone the agency and cancel that booking?

(<u>ANN shakes her head and covers her face with her hands</u>).

MAURICE: All right - I'll phone them myself.

(<u>He goes to the phone and looks in the book for the number.</u>
<u>ANN runs to him and grabs his arm</u>).

ANN (<u>hysterically</u>): No - Maurice - please! I've bought some new things specially for the holiday - <u>please</u> -

MAURICE: ·With whose money?

ANN: Mine, of course - that mother left me -

(<u>MAURICE pushes her away from him and ANN collapses on to the settee</u>).

(<u>DAVID comes in from the kitchen, drinking beer</u>).

DAVID (<u>coldly</u>): At it again, you two? Mum, where's my blue blazer?

ANN (<u>calming down</u>): At the cleaners. It'll be back tomorrow.

DAVID: Hell - I wanted to wear it <u>now</u>.

ANN: Sorry, love -

DAVID: I wish you'd bloody ask me before you send my things to the cleaners.

ANN: I'm <u>sorry</u> -

(<u>MAURICE dials a number and ANN bursts into tears</u>).

Fig. 18.1   *Specimen layout for a stage play*

the ears and the imagination alone: that's the difference. Each sequence must flow into the one that follows, leaving no doubt in the listener's mind as to where and when the action is taking place. The identity of the characters must be unmistakable at all times, so beware of creating characters which are too much alike; two young men or two young women can be confusing unless you devise some obvious difference of temperament or vernacular. Avoid strong dialect; regional speech may be suggested by a turn of phrase but be sure you are really familiar with the region you choose (see Chapter 10).

Your play must be written with a keen visual sense. The listener will have a clear mental image if you write your speeches well; for instance, *'What a lovely dress – I've always adored red velvet.' 'Just look at that moon – I'm sure it's twice its usual size!'* You must also be aware of atmosphere – scents and feelings that bring the scene to life for the listener. (*'Oh, that lilac – I can smell it from here.' 'Tom – your socks need washing!' 'What's that hole in the floor? It looks as if a rat might come out at any moment.'*)

Every sequence should end with a 'fade' or a 'cut'. The passage of time may be indicated by music, silence or some other device of your own invention. Sequences may vary in length from only a few seconds to several minutes, depending on the content; this is one of the ways in which you can introduce variety, along with change of pace, volume of sound, exterior and interior settings – and above all contrasts in character. Time your play by reading it aloud and 'walking through it'. It must fit into one of the available slots, but write it a minute or two too long to allow for trimming in rehearsal. It should on no account be too short; cutting is much easier than inserting new material.

Listen to radio plays as often as possible – and not only the ones you admire. Study the technique with great attention, making notes as you listen. Time the length of the sequences and analyse the ways in which they lead from one to another. It is very useful to listen to a play a second time. It is easier to examine it critically when you are not being carried along by the story.

Example 1

DONALD: I'll see you tomorrow, then – half twelve on the little bridge by the church.

JOAN: Yes – I'll bring a picnic.

DONALD: Suppose it rains?

JOAN: Misery! It won't rain.

(FADE TO SOUND OF HEAVY RAIN)

DONALD: What did I tell you!

The scene is unmistakably changed to the next day on the bridge.

Example 2

MUM: Where's our Meg? It's after ten.

DAD: (Angrily) If she's playing darts with that Joe Scott again, I'll half kill her.

(CUT TO SOUND OF DARTS HITTING DARTBOARD)

MEG: Come on, Joe – you can do better than that.

Example 3

BERYL: We're all at the mercy of our moods. There's nothing we can do about it.

JAMES: Nonsense, darling. There's plenty you can do if you really make an effort.

BERYL: What do *you* know about it? I'll ask Dr Wells this afternoon.

(FADE TO)

BERYL: Doctor, may I ask you something? My husband says you can do something about your moods if you 'make an effort' as he puts it. But you can't, can you? It's all tied up with glands and things, isn't it?

Note that it is essential to insert 'this afternoon' in Beryl's second speech, otherwise the time would not be clearly established; it might be a week or a month later.

An understanding of the precise difference between 'fade' and 'cut' is not important at this stage so long as your story is clearly expressed; the producer will deal with such details once your play is accepted. Keep your sound effects to an absolute minimum. The opening and closing of a door need only be mentioned if someone slams it in a rage or it creaks open stealthily at dead of night. Beware, too, of the sounds of drinks being poured. If it's poison, *then* let us hear it! (This is an exaggeration, but it makes the point.) Amateur writers often make their characters perform actions which cannot register on the air except in long, unexplained silences; they forget that the listener can't see what is happening. Avoid 'stage directions'; any important movements should be written into the dialogue (e.g. 'David – for God's sake – you're doing ninety!' rather than 'David accelerates the car to ninety miles an hour' which would be useless in a radio script). You could introduce a narrator who conveys information to the listener but it would be best to avoid this method for your first play as it is all too easy to overdo the narrator's role and find yourself with a semi-dramatised short story instead of a radio play. Never use a narrator unless there is no other way of writing your play effectively.

Study the *Radio Times* for current requirements. Plays can be of thirty, forty-five, sixty, seventy-five or ninety minutes duration but thirty minutes is probably the most suitable length for your first attempt. See Fig. 18.2 for a specimen layout. The BBC has compiled a booklet entitled *Notes on Radio Drama* which is revised from time to time and deserves careful study. Apply to The Script Editor, Drama (Radio), Broadcasting House, London W1A 1AA. BBC Radio play scripts are also available for study purposes. (Details from BBC Publications, 35 Marylebone High Street, London W1M 4AA.)

Television drama

You may perhaps be disappointed to find so short a section on this important subject, but it is a painful truth that very few writers achieve success with a television play until they are known as novelists or as playwrights in some other field. Some TV companies, in fact, will only consider scripts if they are submitted through a literary agent; this is understandable in view of the high fees paid for television plays and the vast number of hopeful beginners who would otherwise bombard them with unprofessional material. It would therefore be misleading for me to imply that a novice might 'teach

---

(Speeches start numbering from 1 at the top of each page).

1. MARY: It's no good fuming and raging like that, Daddy. Why don't you do something practical about it? Call a public meeting or something?

2. JIM: A public meeting? Yes — all right — that's a good idea, Mary. I'll get some posters printed. Yes — a public meeting...

   (FADE TO SOUNDS OF CHATTERING AND CHAIR-SCRAPING IN THE VILLAGE HALL BEFORE THE MEETING STARTS. OCCASIONAL SNATCHES ARE HEARD: 'Quite a turn-up'; 'Hope they keep it short'; 'About time something was done'. THERE IS A SHARP KNOCKING ON A TABLE AND THE BABBLE DIES DOWN).

3. JIM: Good evening, everybody. And welcome. I'm sure we can all agree about these heavy lorries. It's not like politics and that kind of thing — it's entirely for the good of the community —

   (LAUGHTER)

   I'll ask my daughter to explain our plan for some positive action to keep these damned juggernauts away from our village. Mary?

   (APPLAUSE)

4. MARY: (<u>Brightly</u>) Hello everyone. Before I begin I'd like to take this opportunity of paying tribute to the good work done by —

5. MAN: Cut the cackle, sweetheart — let's get on with it.

   (MURMURS OF PROTEST)

6. WOMAN: Yeah — shut up and let the lady explain.

7. MARY: Thank you. I just wanted to thank the councillors who so kindly arranged for us to use this hall for our meeting and —

8. SAME MAN: I still say out the cackle. What the hell can <u>we</u> do to change the law? And of <u>course</u> it's political. Your father wants his head examined if he thinks any different...

   (A BABBLE OF MINGLED AGREEMENT AND DISSENT)

9. JIM: I didn't want to bring politics into it — it always creates bad feeling. Sorry, Mary — the platform's yours.

Fig. 18.2   *Specimen layout for a radio play*

himself' to write television drama from a book such as this, although the door is open to anyone with special talent who is prepared to master the technique. If you have leanings in this direction, I suggest that you read every available textbook on the subject (books by Janet Dunbar, Malcolm Hulke, Eric Paice and Arthur Swinson are listed in my bibliography) and also perhaps take a correspondence course. In addition you should watch a great deal of television drama, analyse the construction, and keep up to date with new developments, new trends, new possibilities. If you write a play of today make certain that every detail is of *now* and not last year. It is an up-to-the-minute story that has the best chance.

Television plays must, of course, be written specially for the medium. There's no need to worry too much about the technicalities of production and camera work, although you should understand something of what goes on in studio and on location. As with all other forms of drama, it is the strength of the theme, the characterisation and the story-line which will alert a producer to your potential. And if you can turn out a piece of work which is not only well written but also shines out as genuinely *different*, yet without pretentiousness or gimmickry, you may well see your play produced on the small screen even though you are comparatively inexperienced. An original approach is perhaps the most valuable asset any writer has to offer.

Remember to be economical in your settings. Most TV plays are produced in a studio (in some cases with short location film inserts) and four to six sets is a usual maximum. Don't ask for a large elaborate set for one short scene. If you want a palatial drawing room with chandeliers and fabulous furnishings let most of your action take place there. When scenes are shot on film cameras in real locations they are not only costly to produce but demand special writing techniques. You would be wise to make a careful study of one or more of the textbooks available before you plan your play. *Writing for Television* by Malcolm Hulke (A. & C. Black) is packed with information and very readable, even if you have no such aspirations.

It is no use sending the typescript of an unpublished novel

to a television company in the hope that it will be accepted for dramatisation, but there is no harm in offering a *published* novel as a basis for a play or a serial. However, don't be too disappointed if they tell you that they already have similar material under consideration.

Television drama comes under three main headings: the one-off play, the series and the serial. Single plays may last for thirty, sixty or ninety minutes and would offer by far the best opening for a novice. A serial, of course, presents a continuous narrative, each episode ending on a note of suspense, whereas the series consists of several plays written around the same theme, each one complete in itself. Many series also have a strong serial theme running through them, that is, they can only be transmitted in a given order of episodes. Series and serials are often recorded long before they are put out so it's no use trying to write an episode for one you have seen, without previous consultation with the company concerned; professionals are usually commissioned to write them. Serials, however, are sometimes written entirely by one author and this is something you might attempt, although I would strongly advise you to begin with a single play. Series and serials have often to be written – or rewritten – to a very tight schedule, requiring the author to work all through the night to meet a vital deadline. You can appreciate that this is no kind of job for a beginner!

Roy Russell, author of many successful television drama scripts, has this valuable advice to offer: '*A commercially-oriented play is one that has a strong story and fascinating characters. Series episodes are really plays, and their entertainment value is heightened not diminished if the writer is also trying to make an underlying point intrinsic to the story and the characters.*'

Presentation of manuscripts

Plays for stage, radio and television require their own special lay-outs (see Figs 18.1, 18.2 and 18.3). In all cases use A4 paper and isolate the names of the characters in a separate column, using capital letters and typing each name *in full* throughout the script. Initials or abbreviations are not acceptable as they are confusing to anyone who has not read the play before. The speeches should be in single spacing with double spacing between. Stage directions (or for radio, sound effects) must be clearly distinguishable from the speeches and should be typed in capitals and/or underlined. The important thing is that the words to be spoken should stand out unmistakably. (Some books recommend the use of red type for the names of characters and directions but the trouble with this is that red becomes black when the script is duplicated!)

On the title page you must state the running time, carefully estimated by reading it aloud and allowing for pauses and actions. As a very rough guide, you can take it that an A4 page of dialogue such as Fig. 18.2 will play between a minute and a minute and a half, but a page of short speeches will obviously play faster than one with a couple of long speeches, owing to the lay-out.

You should attach a brief synopsis of the play, about 200 words written in the present tense as most synopses are: *Martin Roberts, 55, is awakened in the middle of the night by a phone call from his estranged wife, Laura, who left him five years earlier for another man. She says she is phoning from a local call box and will be with him in a few minutes. He has never ceased to love her and* . . . etc. You should also provide a brief list of characters with a short description of each: for example, ROBIN JONES: a retired architect: LUCY RADCLIFFE: a hairdresser, aged 18. For television you should give a list of sets, describing each one briefly (Set 1: a shoe shop; Set 2: an Italian-style patio). When you type a television play, as you will see in Fig. 18.3, you must only use the right-hand half of the page. The left-hand half is for camera instructions and need not concern you. Don't be intimidated by the complex techniques; it's the story and the dialogue that count. Nevertheless, you should, as always, take care to present your work in a professional manner.

A brief covering letter and return postage should be enclosed when submitting a play of any kind.

SCENE 3. INT. LIVING ROOM. DAY

THE ROOM IS QUITE SMALL, COMFORTABLE,
CHEAPLY FURNISHED, UNTIDY. IVY'S SISTER
JOSIE IS SITTING ON THE FLOOR, SEWING A
LONG SKIRT. SHE IS OLDER THAN IVY, THIN,
SERIOUS, RATHER MASCULINE. IVY IS LYING
ON THE SOFA WITH HER SHOES OFF, EATING
CHOCOLATE.

IVY: I still can't see why she didn't <u>tell</u>
me. It always comes back to that, doesn't it?

JOSIE: She'll have her reasons. Why must you
always nose into people's affairs?

IVY: But I used to be sort of engaged to him.
I must have told you - tall with flaming red
hair. His father was a doctor. Don't you
<u>remember</u>?

JOSIE: Of course I don't remember - it's
donkey's years ago. Why do you always expect
me to remember your things? You don't
remember mine.

(IVY IGNORES THIS; SHE IS SLOW TO TAKE OFFENCE)

IVY: I can't see why Mandy didn't tell me. I'd
have thought she'd be proud of it, marrying
Dennis Fogg. He was a real dish. Though I
must say he frightened us all to death with
his guns.

JOSIE: (LOOKING UP IN ALARM) <u>Guns</u>?

IVY: He was mad about air guns - always
shooting birds and rabbits. I hated that, of
course, but he was a crack shot. Won masses
of things at fairs. Once he tried to make poor
Mandy let him shoot an apple off her head. She
was <u>terrified.</u> He said he was going to tie her
to a tree and -

JOSIE: Bloody sadist! I loathe men like that.

IVY: Yes, well, he did torment us. But boys
do, don't they? They like to frighten girls -
it makes them feel powerful.

JOSIE: Some do, some don't. That's what life's
all about, if you ask me. To hurt or not to
hurt.

(JOSIE TAKES OFF HER SLACKS AND TRIES ON THE
SKIRT)

JOSIE: (CONT) Ronnie never hurt anybody.

Fig. 18.3   *Specimen layout for a television play*

Exercise 18

Write the first five minutes (carefully timed) of either a stage, radio or television play, together with a brief synopsis of the story and a list of characters. In the case of a stage or TV play, give also a list of sets.

19

Finding Titles

Some titles are easy to find, especially those for books of non-fiction which require only a plain statement of the subject (*Cooking for One*; *The Kon-Tiki Expedition*; *Make Your Own Classical Guitar*; *Creative Writing*). The titles of magazine articles should also indicate the subject and avoid ambiguity, but they must obviously be chosen to attract the reader's attention as he turns the pages. They can be simple and direct, making their impact by way of interesting subject matter (*New Developments in Acupuncture*; *Herbs for Your Window-Sill*) or they can be catchy and humorous, probably using puns or alliteration. For instance, if you wrote a light-hearted article on bad driving you might call it *How to Drive your Darling Up the Wall*.

The titles for short stories depend a great deal on the market. A woman's glossy magazine or a literary journal will use straightforward titles such as *The Mirror* or *The New Housekeeper* whereas a romantic weekly might prefer to grab its readers with *Her Summer Secret* or *Roberta's Revenge*. Editors, I'm afraid, will sometimes change your title without consulting you; this is one of the irritations we have to accept. You may, in some cases, prefer the new title, but if you don't there's nothing much you can do. You probably won't even know about it until the magazine is on the bookstalls!

The title of a novel is quite a different matter. It makes a stronger impact on the reader than a short-story title and it will certainly not be changed without your agreement. It's important to find one which is arresting, unusual and perfectly in tune with the book. Sometimes the title comes first, expressing your theme and sparking off a whole novel. The perfect word or phrase will suddenly flash into your mind, straight from heaven, so that you cry out, 'Yes – that's *it!*' More often, however, the book is complete except for the title and you can think of nothing that pleases you.

Key words, I think, might help. Write down as many words as you can think of which relate to your novel – the theme, the main characters, the setting, the climax – and juggle them around until something promising occurs to you. Failing that, look up your key words in a dictionary of quotations or *Roget's Thesaurus* and see if you come across something appropriate. Don't be tempted to use a quotation, however, unless it really fits. And be sure that the title you choose is right for the *mood* of your story.

The notion of paradox can inspire an attractive title (*A Bouquet of Barbed Wire*; *Nuns and Soldiers*; *A Raging Calm*). One-word titles can be strong and effective (*Endgame*; *Airport*; *Praxis*; *Lamb*) and one word with the definite article has produced a wealth of excellent titles (*The Bell*; *The Lie*; *The Comforters*; *The Waterfall*). Many novelists find names for their books in a phrase which describes the main character (*The French Lieutenant's Woman*; *Our Man in Havana*; *Dear Laura*; *Lucky Jim*). Long titles can be fascinating (*The Loneliness of the Long Distance Runner*) but remember they are difficult to fit onto the spine of the book, particularly if your name is also a long one.

Titles for children's books present the usual problems, but you might keep a special eye on the kind of words which youngsters find appealing. A few that come to mind are: Danger, Treasure, Secret, Rescue, Monster, Ghost, Cave and Escape. My own most successful book was a novel for young adults called *Escape on Monday*. I suppose we all want to escape from *something* – and specially on a Monday! That title took a lot of finding but it was well worth the effort.

What about plays? In many ways the same criteria apply as for novels and yet I feel there is a subtle difference which I can't quite put my finger on. (Perhaps *you* can?) One thing is certain: don't choose a long title for a stage play; one day someone might have to put it up in lights!

There is no copyright in titles but it is in your own interest, as well as that of the other author, to avoid duplication. 'How does one find out what's been used before?' you may ask. Bearing in mind that there are about 30 000 new books published in Great Britain every year and 85 000 in the USA, it would be well-nigh impossible to keep track of all those in print, never mind the ones which are out of print but still in the libraries. However, the final decision need not be taken until the book is accepted, and then you can talk the matter over with your publisher.

Exercise 19

Choose alternative titles for any three well-known novels or plays.

20

Editors, Publishers and Literary Agents

Editors

The aspiring writer, sending out manuscripts and waiting in trepidation for the postman to bring them back, is sometimes inclined to develop a sort of persecution mania after a long succession of rejections. One certainly feels helpless; the editorial staff decides what is to be published, and the rejected author has no right to query or complain.

On the other hand, one has only to put oneself in the editor's place to understand that many writers are bound to be disappointed. Some magazines receive hundreds of unsolicited manuscripts a week, and out of that number only a small proportion is up to publication standard. Staff writers and regular contributors provide a good deal of the material and there is also a reserve of accepted freelance work to draw upon.

This does not mean to say that contributions from unknown writers are not of great importance; editors are constantly on the lookout for promising newcomers, and every manuscript is carefully considered. A practised eye, however, can see from the first page – sometimes from the first sentence – whether or not a short story or an article is well written. There are a great many unpublishable manuscripts around; many beginners have no idea how much technical skill and hard work are needed in order to produce a saleable piece of work.

Editors have a very difficult and exhausting job. Most of them understand the problems and the heartaches of the novice and do all they can to encourage new talent and ease the disappointment of those who lack the necessary skills. It is quite impossible, however, in the vast majority of cases for them to state the reasons for refusal. As I have said before, there simply isn't time.

There are, in general, two types of rejection slip: the usual printed one which thanks you for having submitted the MS and regrets that the magazine is unable to publish it, and the personal letter which tells you why your piece is unsuitable and says that the editor would be interested to see some more of your work. *This should give you great encouragement.* Editors do not urge you to submit material unless they like your style. If you receive such a letter, study the market with added zeal and persevere until you receive an acceptance.

When you find a returned manuscript lying on the mat – a bulky envelope instead of the hoped-for thin one – bear in mind that it has not *necessarily* been rejected because it is not good enough. The editor may recently have accepted an article or story on a similar theme, your piece may in some way be in conflict with editorial policy or there could be a personal reason why that particular editor does not find it acceptable.

You must be confident, hard-working and resilient to succeed in the tough competitive world of magazine publishing. If you can picture yourself in an editorial chair, faced every morning with a mountain of manuscripts, many of them the wrong length, ungrammatical, badly typed with the pages unnumbered and copious alterations scribbled illegibly in the margins, you will understand the difficulties. Be patient. Don't enquire about your manuscript until at least two months have elapsed, never telephone an editor or seek an appointment (unless you are a regular contributor) and be sure that your work is right for the market in length, subject and style.

Writers and editors need each other all the time. The writer, while bearing in mind that he must supply outstanding material, should never lose sight of the fact that the editor could not produce a single copy of a magazine without his authors.

Publishers

Publishers, like editors, come in for occasional abuse from writers. I think it has something to do with power. Nobody likes to feel that he is a helpless pawn in any game and the novice can hardly escape that feeling when he sends the typescript of his first book to a publisher. We are all inclined to resist authority (especially the writer, who is often a strong individualist and a bit of a rebel by nature) and we hate to be in a position of such total subservience. ('Who does he think he is, not accepting my book!')

The publisher, like the editor, is continually faced with an avalanche of amateur typescripts, any one of which might be a work of genius but most of which are not. If every writer would send a preliminary letter before dispatching a parcel (see page 83) there would be far fewer cases of stress and distress among both publishers and authors.

You know all about the writer's problems; now let's have a look at the problems of the publisher. It costs thousands of pounds to publish and distribute a book and so he must obviously feel confident of making reasonable sales before he accepts a manuscript. With constantly mounting production costs few publishers can afford to gamble as they might once have done. It's up to you, as the writer, to study your craft and work diligently to produce a book which is so original, so readable and so professionally organised that the publisher you choose (and your choice must be a wise one) will see it as an attractive business proposition as well as a work of art.

If your manuscript is refused, with no reason given except that their 'lists are full', don't be discouraged. Many successful books were sent to more than a dozen publishers before they were accepted, including *Room at the Top*, *Catch 22* and *Watership Down*. My own *Craft of Novel-Writing* went to twenty-six and was then published simultaneously in hardback and paperback. Provided you are confident that the book is as good as you can make it, keep on trying and at last you may receive the letter you dream of.

Let's assume that you have in fact received that letter. A publisher likes your book and is prepared to offer you a contract. He will probably suggest a meeting at this stage so that you can get to know one another over lunch and discuss the book. If you are a new writer he will want to hear about your future plans, so think them out before you see him.

The next thing is for him to draw up a contract which will eventually be signed by both of you. (If you employ a literary agent he will have his own form of contract.) The contract is a legal document setting out the points which must be agreed before the book can be published, notably the percentage of the selling price which you will receive. (You should never sell the copyright of your book for a lump sum; few publishers would expect it. See page 134.) You will probably be offered from ten to fifteen per cent on the hardback edition, depending on the number of copies sold (perhaps ten per cent for the first 2500, twelve for the next 2500 and fifteen thereafter). These percentages will vary according to the publisher, the type of book and your professional standing.

Royalties may be assessed as a simple percentage of the published price or on the publisher's receipts which means the published price less the trade discount (which ranges from thirty to fifty per cent). Royalties on export and paperback sales are specified separately and are usually at a lower rate. If all this seems confusing, don't worry – it *is* confusing! If you employ an agent you can forget about it and let him do the worrying.

On signature of the contract you will receive the first instalment of your 'advance'. This is a sum of money which is usually non-returnable (thank goodness!) and which represents an advance on royalties. This means that until this sum has been repaid by early sales you will receive no further monies. It is usual to be paid half the advance on signature and half on publication If the book has been commissioned on the strength of a synopsis and two or three chapters, you may expect a third of your advance on signature, a third on delivery of the typescript and a third on publication. In this case the required length of the book and the delivery date will also be stipulated in the contract. Never promise a date which you can't fulfil, but if, through unforeseen circumstances, you require a postponement, let your publisher know in good time so that he can reorganise his schedule.

Your book will probably take about a year to appear in print, but six months or so after the delivery of your final manuscript, the proofs will arrive for correction. You are allowed about two weeks to check them carefully for printing errors. This is *not* the time to revise your book! Your typescript must be as near perfect as you can make it before it goes to the printers. Proof corrections are expensive and there will be a clause in your contract committing you to pay for any corrections of your own above a certain amount. (Printers' mistakes, of course, are not your responsibility except for spotting them!) Proof correcting should hold no fears for you; the *Writers' and Artists' Yearbook* gives clear instructions on the use of the correct symbols.

Never pay to have a book (except perhaps of poetry) published; if your manuscript is worthy of publication, sooner or later it will be accepted and royalties paid in the normal way. An unscrupulous 'vanity' publisher will praise your book to the skies and make impossible promises in order to persuade you to part with your money.

When you become a published author, with all the joys and traumas allied to success, you will have to face the problem of book jackets. Many novelists (myself included) have had just cause for complaint. One can sympathise with the jacket artist who cannot be expected to read every book from cover to cover, but factual errors could be avoided if the author received a 'rough' of the jacket before the final artwork was prepared. This, in my opinion, should be common practice, not a grudging concession we have to fight for. I have always insisted on this being done, and on several occasions I have found serious mistakes and had them corrected. When the original design goes to press without being vetted (as many do) the author comes in for a share of the criticism if something is wrong; people often think that authors choose their own jackets and are to blame if they are badly designed, erroneous or vulgar.

Finally, remember that the author's relationship with his publisher is a very delicate one. We all long for the ideal publisher who will appreciate the hard work we do, understand our problems, produce our books in a beautiful format with a superb jacket, advertise widely, provide regular sales figures, pay up on time – and accept our next book without a quibble.

The publisher, I think, must dream of the following virtues in his authors: neatness and accuracy, punctual delivery of MSS and corrected proofs, a minimum of letters and phone calls, a good-humoured professional approach and, last but not least, a regular output of highly marketable books!

Literary Agents

If you were to eavesdrop on two successful authors there's every chance that they would be talking about their agents. And it would probably be quite a heated discussion:

> *'My agent is hopeless. He takes my ten per cent and does absolutely nothing for me. He never answers my letters and now that I want to leave him I can't get my manuscripts back.'*
>
> *'Really? Oh, I'm terribly lucky. Mine couldn't be more helpful. She's earned me thousands over the years . . .'*

So how do you go about finding a reliable agent?

The wisest approach is to go by personal recommendation, but if you are out of touch with professional writers you should refer to the *Writers' and Artists' Yearbook.*

Many authors manage quite well without an agent but if you are a dreamy kind of person with no business sense, I think you would be well advised to look for one. (I'm only talking about books and plays; few agents are interested in articles or short stories by beginners.)

Let's consider the advantages of employing an agent:

1   He knows the most suitable publishers for your particular manuscript and will send it out (many times, if need be) at no extra cost. You don't pay him a penny until he has found you a publisher and then he will deduct the usual ten per cent plus VAT from your royalties. Avoid any agent who charges a reading fee.

2   He will draw up a fair contract, doing battle with your publisher, if necessary, to secure better terms.

3   He will explore the possibilities of paperback rights,

serial rights, radio and television rights, and so on. Having contacts in many parts of the world, he is in an ideal position to negotiate foreign rights.

4   He will look after your financial interests, making sure that you receive payment on time.

5   He will advise you on all matters connected with your work, although he cannot be expected to do more than minor editing.

6   Manuscripts received from a reputable agent are often put at the top of the pile on a publisher's desk. All manuscripts are given careful consideration in due course, but if you employ an agent you might well receive priority treatment.

7   Knowing your abilities, he might obtain a commission for you to write a book.

It is not always easy for a new writer to find an agent who is prepared to take him on; naturally, your manuscript must appeal to him as a marketable commodity. Choose an agent who specialises in your type of work (see the *Yearbook*) and send a preliminary letter describing your book very briefly and asking if he would be willing to consider it. If you receive a favourable reply, send him your manuscript, making sure that it has a good professional appearance and enclosing return postage.

If he is not prepared to take you on, he will probably tell you why your book falls short of his requirements. You should take careful note of his comments and consider revising your work accordingly. Don't spoil your chances of success for the want of a little humility. I've seen it happen too often.

If you are successful in finding an agent, don't keep badgering him about the fate of your manuscript. Leave him to send it out as he thinks fit; he will let you know at once if he has good news for you. He will expect to handle all your subsequent work and this is as it should be. You can look forward to many years of friendly cooperation with a business representative who has your interests very much at heart. After all, his livelihood depends on the success of his authors.

21

Writers' Circles

All over the country there are writers with talent and ideas but insufficient knowledge of how to shape their work for publication. Guidebooks such as this can help, of course, but many beginners are battling on alone with no one to point out their faults or offer encouragement. Sometimes there is a relative or friend who says how lovely their stories are (or what rubbish!) but often there is no one at all to take an interest.

Creative Writing classes are perhaps the best solution but they are not always available. (You can find out from your public library.) Conferences, lectures and correspondence courses can be very helpful but the answer for you – unless you are a born loner – could be to join the nearest Writers' Circle. Most of these can boast a few experts but in any case you will learn a lot from other amateurs; a fresh eye can often spot mistakes you have overlooked. For anyone who is not afraid of criticism, a local group can be the beginning of success. It was for me.

Serious writers often leave a circle because it turns out to be a mere social gathering, a cosy get-together for gossip and mutual admiration. It's up to the chairman (and those who elect him) to see that this doesn't happen. The chairman should also ensure that articles and stories provoke discussion on the quality of the writing, not on the subject matter, otherwise an article on blood sports, for example, might create bad feeling. A happy atmosphere is vital if the group is to thrive.

If there is no circle in your area (again you can find out at the public library), you could start one yourself by placing an advertisement in your local paper. Make it clear that beginners are welcome and ask for those who are interested to get in touch. You may only have a few members at the outset but your group will grow if it is efficiently and cheerfully run.

Here are a few points to consider:

1 When will you meet?

Fortnightly is a good compromise, though some circles meet every week. If possible you should keep going throughout the year without a break; summer recesses can ruin good resolutions.

I suggest a weekday evening, from 7.30 to 10.00. Married writers often need to be diplomatic and I wouldn't advise the weekend. Arrange a definite time to start and then meet fifteen minutes earlier for a warming-up chat. Once the meeting has begun the group should concentrate entirely on writing matters.

2 A room

Schools, libraries, church halls, social clubs and back rooms in pubs or hotels are the usual venue. As a last resort you might have to meet in each other's houses to begin with, but this has the disadvantage of encouraging chit-chat rather than serious work. Curtains are admired, photographs passed round and recipes exchanged; small wonder that male writers sometimes decide that a circle is not for them! Another argument against meeting in private houses is that it provokes competition over the standard of refreshments provided. It may also cause embarrassment to those who, for one reason or another, are unable to provide hospitality.

3 The subscription

This will depend on the cost of the premises, but it should be kept as low as possible. Charge an additional small contribution for each session to build up funds for professional speakers, competition prizes, social events and so on.

4 The members

In my view, anyone with a sincere desire to improve his or her work should be eligible to join. Publication ought never to be a condition of membership because Writers' Circles exist to help people into print. Nobody who works hard and welcomes criticism should feel unworthy to belong. There are many unpublished manuscripts of great merit and many published ones of little merit. Originality, enthusiasm and perseverance are the qualities I most admire in the members of my group, irrespective of commercial success. In any case, today's unpublished writers can be the best-sellers of tomorrow.

As for age, many groups have members ranging from eighteen to eighty. I know a lady who sold her first article at the age of seventy-six. She was wise enough to profit from the advice of fellow writers.

5 The chairman

He or she should really be a professional writer, but it is of prime importance that this office be held by someone who can deal firmly but pleasantly with anyone who talks too much or out of turn. Shy people must be encouraged to participate in the criticism of manuscripts and this can be achieved by asking them what they liked most and least about a piece of work. Criticism should be detailed and outspoken but never discouraging. It should be on as deep a level as possible with special attention to construction. Possible markets should be suggested if the work is considered saleable.

All comments should be noted down by the author and analysed at leisure; some may be acted upon, others discounted, but every opinion should receive respectful attention. We all feel sensitive about our work but those who are nervous of criticism often grow braver when they see other members accepting it gratefully, acting upon it and selling their work as a result.

6 Competitions

Circle meetings encourage a regular output of work but competitions with book-token prizes provide an added incentive. Articles, short stories, radio talks, character studies or the first three pages of a novel, play or non-fiction book make suitable categories. It is a good idea to set a choice of two subjects – one fiction and one non-fiction. Some of the exercises in this book might be useful. A maximum length should be stipulated and it is as well to emphasise that typescripts must be neatly presented. Entries should be anonymous and the winner may be chosen by a ballot vote or judged by an outside body such as a neighbouring Writers' Circle.

It takes initiative and effort to start a group – or even to join an existing one – but it can lead to a new life of creativity, additional income and many lasting friendships.

22

The Professional Approach

It may be that you have no interest in the commercial aspect of writing and only want to enjoy it as a private leisurely activity, just for the love of it. This chapter is intended, as the heading implies, for those who have already seen their work in print or hope to do so one day.

When you are a beginner you are inclined to worry about matters which cease to trouble you when you become established. If you are still a novice, a few words of advice at this stage might help you to avoid those anxieties.

Try not to fret if a magazine spells your name wrongly, changes the title of your story, omits a vital paragraph or makes a printing error that gives the impression that you are illiterate! For years I used to be upset about such things, wasting nervous energy that might have been used creatively. At last, mainly through contact with professional writers, I learned to shrug off minor irritations, realising that almost every writer has similar problems. Nevertheless, you must be firm in your complaint if you have a real grievance. An important aspect of the professional approach is to know when to take a stand and when to 'let it ride'.

Twelve points for new writers

1 Attend to the advice of editors and publishers with respect; it is usually valid.
2 Keep your letters and phone calls as brief as possible.

3   Don't mention personal problems if you can possibly avoid it.

4   Never drop in on your agent or publisher without an appointment.

5   Let them know if you are going to be away for more than a week.

6   Answer letters promptly.

7   Be sure that your typescripts are beyond reproach.

8   Always enclose return postage when you submit a manuscript. If you send material overseas enclose sufficient International Reply Coupons to cover return postage by airmail or surface – one coupon is not usually enough even for a short article by air. These are obtainable from any Post Office.

9   Be accurate and up to date in all your facts.

10   Don't send out the same piece to more than one editor at the same time. (I should point out here that in exceptional circumstances – with topical material, for instance – a book may be sent to more than one publisher simultaneously. It must be stated that other publishers are also being approached but there is no need to say who they are.)

11   Don't be in a hurry to send out your work before you have revised it sufficiently.

12   Don't forget that guidelines – even those given in this book – are no more than the name implies. They can be immensely helpful to the novice, but should not be followed too rigidly.

When you begin to achieve some success you should consider joining the Society of Authors (84 Drayton Gardens, London SW10) or the Writers' Guild of Great Britain (430 Edgware Road, London W2). Write to both for details and decide which you prefer. (American writers should contact the Authors' Guild/Authors' League at 234 West 44th Street, New York, NY 10036.) In my opinion it is incumbent upon every practising writer to belong, not only for the tremendous benefits (including the vetting of contracts) but also because we must band together to defend our rights. Authors, unless they are extremely successful, receive a pitifully low income compared with most other professions, and they are helpless to improve matters if they work alone.

As a would-be professional you will want to understand the rulings on income tax, copyright, libel and so on. Excellent articles on these matters can be found in our indispensable ally, the current *Writers' and Artists' Yearbook*. The laws are much too complex for me to explain in detail, but it might be helpful if I touch briefly on some aspects as they concern the novice. You can extend your knowledge when you need to do so.

Libel

This is vaguely worrying for every published writer. We shall obviously write nothing which we *know* to be libellous but how can we be sure that some complete stranger, bearing the same name as the villain of one of our novels, will not sue us for defamation of character? We can't. We can only take reasonable precautions by checking the telephone book for the area in which the story is set, or even contacting the local Post Office to make sure that no one of that name is resident there. The well-known statement that 'the characters in this book are entirely fictitious and bear no resemblance to any actual person, alive or dead' carries no legal protection but it might deter a would-be troublemaker.

Income tax

This is a matter that will not concern you until you progress beyond the stage of writing as a hobby, but I strongly advise you to keep a careful record of your casual earnings and all your expenses for each financial year. The appropriate receipts should also be preserved. When you become successful, the losses incurred by previous expenses may be carried forward over a certain number of years and deducted from your taxable income. There are many points to consider but if you ask your tax inspector for advice you will usually find him helpful and cooperative in assessing your entitlements.

Copyright

As a general guide, the copyright of an author's writings – even a letter to a friend – belongs to him (or his estate) until fifty years after his death. After that time he may be quoted freely. (If he collaborated with another author, the copyright remains with the one who died last.) There is no copyright in ideas. If someone writes a story which is very similar to one of yours, you have no case for legal action unless it can be proved that the plot itself contains situations which have been deliberately stolen (i.e. plagiarised). It is quite possible for two people to hit on the same idea, even a very unusual one, and new writers are apt to get needlessly upset on this account.

There is also no copyright in facts, but it is illegal to copy the exact words of another author in stating them. That John Keats was born in October 1795 and died in Rome at the age of twenty-five are established facts and anyone may state them, but when a writer expresses a fact in his own individual way (even in an encyclopaedia) his actual words may not be reproduced without permission.

Quotations

If you wish to quote from another author you must obtain written consent from his publisher, agent or whoever handles the quotation rights. Short extracts are usually allowed if they do not constitute 'a substantial part' of the work, which in practice generally means you can quote up to fifty words of prose without asking for consent. In the case of poetry, however, even a single line must be cleared for permission as it may form 'a substantial part' of the whole work. For reviews and serious works of literary criticism longer extracts are allowed, but the rules are complicated and in all forms of writing you should always inform your editor or publisher at the outset if you wish to use quotations, and be guided by him.

In *all* circumstances the quotation must be identified and proper acknowledgment made, so it is very important to note *full* details of all your sources as you go along. Make quite certain, too, that you have quoted accurately, including punctuation.

Permission to quote is seldom refused but a fee may be charged – sometimes quite a large one – and you should always wait for a reply before you commit yourself to a particular quotation. Payment is normally due on publication of the piece in question.

Complimentary copies

Non-writing friends and relatives will sometimes expect you to give them a copy of your latest book, duly inscribed. They do not realise that an author receives only six copies of each title free of charge from his publisher and that he will need to supply copies for his agent to send abroad in quest of foreign rights. You may, however, buy your own books from the publisher at trade price, although not to re-sell them.

The need for perseverance

I think it is usually a mistake to drag out old manuscripts and try to rehash them; it is better to forge ahead with something fresh. You are a more capable person now than you were a year ago. Experience has seen to that: not only practice in writing but the people you have met, the problems you have faced, the stresses and successes, the imaginings. . . . Every experience, good and bad, can help us to become better writers, and that can be a comforting thought when we are going through a difficult patch in our lives.

One of the greatest enemies a novice has to face – and a professional, too, for that matter – is despondency. Our writing is so important to us that strong criticism from colleagues, rejection by editors or publishers, or simply a vague feeling of inadequacy, can be very depressing unless we dig in our heels and vow to persevere in spite of all setbacks. Many best-selling authors had to slog away for years before the breakthrough came; I know a popular television playwright who submitted more than forty scripts before he had one accepted. Keep that in mind if you feel like giving up after two or three rejections!

My last piece of advice is one that I have sometimes ignored myself, with depressing results. *Be single-minded!* Finish what you are doing before you begin something else. If you have problems half way through a novel (and who doesn't?) don't break off and write short stories or start another book. Take a deep breath, pour yourself a stiff drink, say a prayer – or whatever suits you best (I like all three!) – and make up your mind to get that novel right, even if it means going back to the beginning and starting again. Of course, there are occasions when you may genuinely lose interest in a project or realise that you are not yet ready to follow it through. This is rare, I think; the usual reasons for leaving something unfinished are laziness and fear of failure. Overcome these hazards and success will come much sooner.

Anne Sexton, the American poet and playwright, interviewed for the *Paris Review*, was asked what she thought a teacher could give a writer in a Creative Writing class. '*Courage, of course,*' she replied. '*That's the most important ingredient.*'

Later she was asked: '*What is the quality of feeling when you're writing?*'

'*Well, it's a beautiful feeling, even if it's hard work. When I'm writing I know I'm doing the thing I was born to do.*'

I feel like that myself, and I hope it's going to be the same for you.

Bibliography

Walter Allen (ed.), *Writers on Writing*, Phoenix House, London, and E. P. Dutton, New York

Miriam Allott, *Novelists on the Novel*, Routledge and Kegan Paul, London, and Boston, Mass.

William Archer, *Playmaking*, Chapman and Hall, London

William Ash, *The Way to Write Radio Drama*, Elm Tree Books, London

Geoffrey Ashe, *The Art of Writing Made Simple*, William Heinemann, London, and Doubleday & Co. Inc., New York

Donna Baker, *How to Write Stories for Magazines*, Allison and Busby, London

H. E. Bates, *The Modern Short Story*, Michael Joseph, London

Anthony Blond, *The Publishing Game*, Jonathan Cape, London

Victor Bonham-Carter, *Authors by Profession*, Society of Authors, London

Malcolm Bradbury (ed.), *The Novel Today*, Fontana/Collins, London, and Rowman & Littlefield, Totowa, New Jersey

John Braine, *Writing a Novel*, Eyre Methuen, London

Dorothea Brande, *Becoming a Writer*, Macmillan, London

Albert Camus, *Carnets* (2 volumes), Hamish Hamilton, London, and as *Notebooks 1942–1951*, Alfred A. Knopf, New York

R. V. Cassill, *Writing Fiction*, Prentice Hall, New Jersey

Cyril Connolly, *The Unquiet Grave*, Hamish Hamilton, London

Cyril Connolly, *Enemies of Promise*, Penguin Books, London

Brian Cooke, *Writing Comedy for Television*, Methuen, London

Giles Cooper, *Radio Plays*, BBC Publications, London

Christopher Derrick, *Reader's Report*, Victor Gollancz, London

Jill Dick, *Freelance Writing for Newspapers*, A. & C. Black, London

Elizabeth Dipple, *Plot*, Methuen, London

Garry Disher, *Writing Fiction*, Penguin Books, London

Dianne Doubtfire, *The Craft of Novel-Writing*, Allison and Busby, London and New York

Janet Dunbar, *Script Writing for Television*, Museum Press, London

John Fairfax and John Moat, *The Way to Write*, Elm Tree Books, London

Peter Finch, *How to Publish your Poetry*, Allison and Busby, London and New York

E. M. Forster, *Aspects of the Novel*, Edward Arnold, London, and Harcourt, Brace, Jovanovich, New York

Pamela Frankau, *Pen to Paper*, William Heinemann, London

Stuart Griffiths, *How Plays Are Made*, William Heinemann, London

John Herbert, *Radio Journalism*, A. & C. Black, London

John Hines, *The Way to Write Non-Fiction*, Elm Tree Books, London

Ann Hoffmann, *Research for Writers*, A. & C. Black, London

Malcolm Hulke, *Writing for Television*, A. & C. Black, London

Paddy Kitchen, *The Way to Write Novels*, Elm Tree Books, London

Tessa Krailing, *How to Write for Children*, Allison and Busby, London

Michael Legat, *Dear Author*, Pelham Books, London

Michael Legat, *An Author's Guide to Publishing*, Robert Hale,

Michael Legat, *The Nuts and Bolts of Writing*, Robert Hale, London

Michael Legat, *Understanding Publishers' Contracts*, Robert Hale, London

Michael Legat, *Writing for Pleasure and Profit*, Robert Hale, London

R. W. B. Lewis, *The Picaresque Saint*, Victor Gollancz, London

Rhona Martin, *Writing Historical Fiction*, A. & C. Black, London

Somerset Maugham, *A Writer's Notebook*, William Heinemann, London and Arno Press, New York

André Maurois, *The Art of Writing*, Bodley Head, London, and Arno Press, New York

Barry Maybury, *Writers' Workshop*, Batsford, London

Alberto Moravia, *Man as an End*, Secker and Warburg, London, and Farrar, Straus and Giroux Inc., New York

F. A. Mumby and Ian Norrie, *Publishing and Bookselling*, Jonathan Cape, London

Eric Paice, *The Way to Write for Television*, Elm Tree Books, London

Paris Review Interviews, *Writers at Work* (7 volumes) Secker and Warburg, London, and Viking Press Inc., New York

J. B. Priestley, *The Art of the Dramatist*, William Heinemann, London

V. S. Pritchett, *The Working Novelist*, Chatto and Windus, London

Frederic Raphael (ed.), *Bookmarks*, Jonathan Cape, London

Alain Robbe-Grillet. *Towards a New Novel*, John Calder, London, and Grove Press Inc., New York

Ian Rodger, *Radio Drama*, Macmillan, London

Ivan Roe, *A Style of Your Own*, David and Charles, London

Jean Saunders, *The Craft of Writing Romance*, Allison and Busby, London

Jean Saunders, *Writing Step by Step*, Allison and Busby, London

John Steinbeck, *Journal of a Novel*, William Heinemann, London, and Viking Press Inc., New York

Frances Stillman, *The Poet's Manual*, Thames and Hudson, London

William Strunk and E. B. White, *The Elements of Style*, Macmillan, London and New York

Arthur Swinson, *Writing for Television Today*, A. & C. Black, London

Michael Temple, *A Pocket Guide to Written English*, John Murray, London

Margaret Thomson Davis, *The Making of a Novelist*, Allison and Busby, London

Ion Trewin, *Journalism*, David and Charles, London

Stanley Unwin, *The Truth about Publishing*, Allen and Unwin, London, and Winchester, Mass.

G. H. Vallins, *Good English*, Pan Books, London
G. H. Vallins, *Better English*, Pan Books, London

Gordon Wells, *The Craft of Writing Articles*, Allison and Busby, London
Gordon Wells, *The Successful Author's Handbook*, Macmillan, London
Gordon Wells, *The Magazine Writer's Handbook*, Allison and Busby, London and New York
Gordon Wells, *Writers' Questions Answered*, Allison and Busby, London
John Whale, *Put it in Writing*, Dent, London
Mary Wibberley, *To Writers With Love*, Buchan & Enright, London
Angus Wilson, *The Wild Garden*, Secker and Warburg, London, and University of California Press, Berkeley, Calif.
Colin Wilson, *The Craft of the Novel*, Victor Gollancz, London

Index of Authors Quoted

Adams, Richard, 97

Basho, 73
Bates, H. E., 31, 37, 50
Burton, Ian J., 73
Butterfield, Sam, 74

Carrol, Lewis, 52
Chesterton, G. K., 47
Conrad, Joseph, 68

Dahl, Roald, 37
Drabble, Margaret, 59

Eliot, T. S., 74

Fowles, John, 59–60, 93
Fry, Christopher, 71

Gordimer, Nadine, 37, 38
Graves, Robert, 69

Hersey, John, 65
Hopkins, Gerard Manley, 72
Huxley, Aldous, 47

Issa, 73

James, P. D., 49
Johnson, Samuel, 4

Krailing, Tessa, 97–8

Lee, Laurie, 70
Lewis, Cecil Day, 70

McEwan, Ian, 49–50
Monsarrat, Nicholas, 43
Moritake, 73
Murdoch, Iris, 61

O'Brien, Edna, 38
Oliver, Colin, 73
Owen, Wilfred, 70

Paton Walsh, Jill, 95
Pirandello, Luigi, 48
Plath, Sylvia, 70

Russell, Roy, 113
Ryokan, 73

Scannell, Vernon, 70
Sexton, Anne, 136
Shakespeare, William, 71
Stevenson, Robert Louis, 19

Tchekov, Anton, 59
Thomas, Dylan, 70

Watts, Alan, 72

Waugh, Evelyn, 1
Wilder, Thornton, 103
Wright, Dorothy, 67

SPELLING

PATRICK THORNHILL

An indispensable guide for everyone who has to put pen to paper or paper to typewriter.

This book is essential for all uncertain spellers who want a quick way of finding out how a word should be spelt. The author has devised a unique and simple system based on sounds which quickly guides a mis-speller to the correct spelling of a word and its derivatives.

The vocabulary equals that of a medium-sized dictionary. It includes words in everyday use which have not yet found their way into many dictionaries, American spellings, foreign words and phrases in common use, and also some words that are used mainly in Australia and New Zealand.

TEACH YOURSELF BOOKS

CORRECT ENGLISH

B. A. PHYTHIAN

This practical guide and reference handbook will help you improve your own use of English in everyday life and enhance your appreciation of good English writing.

The book first provides handy summaries of the main rules of grammar and punctuation. It then examines some of the more common errors in spoken and written English, before giving practical advice on spelling and helpful definitions of words which are frequently confused and misused.

The second half of the book focuses on the correct and effective use of English in a wide variety of contexts, and illustrates the different types of language and style which contribute to the subtlety and variety of English expression. A particularly useful feature of the book is an extensive guide to the conventions of written English in everyday life, including business and commercial English, letters, reports, summaries and precis, and English for examinations.

TEACH YOURSELF BOOKS

LETTER WRITING

DAVID JAMES

A complete guide to writing letters which say exactly what you want to say — and bring the desired response.

This book explains how to write effective letters. David James offers practical advice on the choice of layout, style and 'tone', and then examines different kinds of letters ranging from the simple thank-you note to the more involved job application or sales letter to a potential customer.

Numerous sample letters illustrate correct forms and common errors, and highlight the various conventions and courtesies observed in different parts of the world. Forms of address and a list of common abbreviations are also included for easy reference, making this a book for every home or office.

TEACH YOURSELF BOOKS